AMERICA AND THE IMAGE OF EUROPE
Reflections on American Thought

AMERICA AND THE IMAGE OF EUROPE

Reflections on American Thought

DANIEL J. BOORSTIN

MERIDIAN BOOKS, INC. *New York*

DANIEL J. BOORSTIN

Daniel J. Boorstin was born in Atlanta, Georgia, on October 1, 1914. He was educated at Harvard; at Oxford, where he took two degrees (he was also admitted to the English bar); and at Yale, where he gained a doctorate in legal history. Now professor of American history at the University of Chicago, Mr. Boorstin is the author of the following books: THE MYSTERIOUS SCIENCE OF THE LAW (*1941*), THE LOST WORLD OF THOMAS JEFFERSON (*1948*), THE GENIUS OF AMERICAN POLITICS (*1953*), *and* THE AMERICANS: THE COLONIAL EXPERIENCE (*1958*), *which was awarded the coveted Bancroft Prize.*

M

AN ORIGINAL MERIDIAN BOOK
Published by Meridian Books, Inc. March 1960
First printing February 1960

A Zen monk horrified his disciple by splitting up a wooden image of the Buddha for kindling. The shocked acolyte asked him why he did it and the answer was "to find the *shari*" (pearls left when the Buddha's body is cremated). "But," protested the boy, "that is sacrilege. Besides, you'll find no *shari* there." At which his master went on chopping wood, saying, "No *shari,* no sacrilege."

Old Buddhist Tale

To Walter Johnson

CONTENTS

FOREWORD

I would like to think that these essays are written
from a point of view that will soon become obsolete. In the next generation, I hope, a comparable
volume would have to be called "America and the
Image of the World." For I hope we will give more
of our thought to locating ourselves not only in
the old map of Europe and her colonies, but also
in a new map of the whole world. We will, I hope,
rise above the level of *homo sapiens Europaeus* to
the level of *homo sapiens*.

Until now when we have started to talk about
the uniqueness of America we have almost always
ended by comparing ourselves to Europe. Toward
her we have felt all the attractions and repulsions
of Oedipus. Only by denying our parent can we
become a truly independent New World; yet we
cannot help feeling that the New World is the fulfillment of a European dream. We are both a
happy non-Europe and a happy afterlife of Europe.
Europe is both our beloved "mother country" and
the pernicious source of all "alien ideologies." We
owe to her our religion, our common law, our ideal

of constitutionalism; but also the ancient menaces of aristocracy, feudalism, and monopoly, and the modern menace of communism.

Few peoples have been so obsessed by a parental image. The Romans were haunted by Greece; but they had not come from Greece, most of them did not speak Greek, and neither the attraction nor the repulsion was so great. Most European nations do not even know from where their first settlers came. We of all modern peoples are dominated by the specter of known foreign ancestors.

The following essays—a product of my effort in recent years to discover what is distinctive in American history—are therefore inevitably concerned with our distinctions from Europe. They are concerned with how the image of Europe has given us our bearings, and yet how un-European is the framework of our life and the pattern of our history: for example, the way we think of neighboring countries, the role of our intellectuals, the style of our historical monuments, the character of our political leadership, and the sources of our discontent. I have been surprised to discover how difficult it still is to describe our uniqueness except by reference to Europe.

Perhaps it is inevitable that we try to distinguish ourselves from our parents before we distinguish ourselves from the whole world. Yet it is time we cease thinking of ourselves as an outpost of Western European civilization. Of course we are ex-colonials, and we have only recently begun to move our cultural capital within our own borders. But we must not doom ourselves to remain an epilogue to European history, making ourselves only a newer Old World. This cannot be avoided unless we learn to treat non-European cultures as equals. Only if we can relate ourselves to, and acquire the new habit of comparing ourselves with, the cultures of Asia and Africa—with China and India, with the Arab nations and the rising peoples of Negro Africa. Only then can we remain part of a New World.

When we first look in the vast mirror of the world, we are apt to lose our bearings. We lose even the sense of our limitations, of which our European relatives have been happy to remind us. We begin to have Dreams of Glory, like those of the child who still thinks that he can at the same time become President of the United States, author of the Great American Novel, and Home Run King of the Big Leagues. We too have had only a brief opportunity to prove our incapacities.

In recent years, as we have become conscious of our great role on the world stage, we have read and written a lot about American life and the American destiny. Much of it expresses the callowness of our not yet having discovered the range of our national incompetence. Most of it expresses the malaise that comes from continuing to judge our culture by irrelevant European standards. All of it expresses the confusion that comes from our pretending to be a World Capital before we have quite ceased to be a province of Europe.

Our attitude toward our own culture has recently been characterized by two qualities, braggadocio and petulance. Braggadocio—empty boasting of American power, American virtue, American know-how—has dominated our foreign relations now for some decades. It is the spirit of making the world safe for democracy, of unconditional surrender, of crusading for the American way of life—in a word, of belief in American omnicompetence. It is the belief that there is nothing we cannot do if we only put more money into it and get organized. Its symbol is Paul Bunyan who, contrary to common belief, is not an ancient figure of our true folklore, but is the invention of men advertising lumber around 1910. We can not only lick the world, we can out-preach them, out-televise them, out-philosophize them, out-democratize them. The humblest expression of this braggart spirit would be the prayer of the Pharisee (in Luke, 18:11): "God, I thank thee that I am not as other men are."

Here at home—within the family, so to speak— our attitude to our culture expresses a superficially different spirit, the spirit of petulance. Never before, perhaps, has a culture been so fragmented into groups, each full of its own virtue, each annoyed and irritated at the others. The sure and familiar formula for a successful nonfiction book, for a novel, a movie, or a television show, is to expose the vices of some occupation, some section, or some class. We are ashamed of our hucksters, our hidden persuaders, our exurbanites, our men-in-gray-flannel-suits, our occupiers of executive suites (and their wives), our organization men, our labor racketeers, our anti-intellectual, TV-watching, comic-book-reading populace, and our ineffectual egghead professors. Adults are horrified by our beatnik youth, and our beatnik youth are horrified by the squares who are us. Northern pulpits resound with outrage at the inhumanity to Negroes of fellow Americans in the South. Southerners are astonished at the anarchistic love of violence of the NAACP and their northern supporters (including the Supreme Court).

Among intellectuals this petulance has been worst of all. For perhaps the first time in American history they have blatantly and with some success declared their separateness from the rest of the nation. The word "intellectual" (and its by-product, "anti-intellectual") has come into use in this country only very recently—in the present century. Among intellectuals at least much of the petulance is based on the surviving assumption that we can and should shape our culture on West European models. That we must Oxfordize our universities, Great-Bookify our reading matter, Left-Bankify our art, Parliamentiarize our politics, Aristocratize our social life, and Salonize our conversation.

What both the braggadocio spirit and the petulant spirit have in common is that they both overestimate our national capacity. They both assume that a great nation like us can do whatever it wishes. They share the illusion of omnicompetence which has haunted every world power. Because we have decent political institutions, a mobile and egalitarian society, a high standard of living, and a literate populace, they say we can also be the world's greatest philosophers, the world's most amusing conversationalists, and the world's best artists. In this national arrogance perhaps our only competitors today are the Soviets, whose illusions of omnicompetence are more dogmatic than ours.

We must try to displace arrogance by self-respect. And self-respect can come only from a clearer image of the extent and the limits of our competence.

To try to see American culture as a whole, to try to balance our failures and our successes can help us sharpen that image. The best clues are in our past, in the kind of thing we have and have not been able to do, in the price we have had to pay for our successes. Paranoia may be engaging in children, it may even be necessary in artists, but it is death to a nation and an offense to the world. To face our own limitations—and those are defined largely by our past—not only helps us economize our energy and our passion. It also helps us discover and respect the whole un-American World.

1. AMERICA AND THE IMAGE OF EUROPE

In the United States until about the beginning of the present century, "American" and "European" were used less as precise geographical terms than as logical antitheses. What Crèvecoeur described was how a man ceased to be a "European" in order to become an "American." When Jefferson traveled in France he saw the "European" contrast to the "American" condition. "We can no longer say there is nothing new under the sun," Jefferson wrote to Priestley on March 21, 1801. "For this whole chapter in the history of man is new. . . . Before the establishment of the American States, nothing was known to history but the man of the old world, crowded within limits either small or overcharged, and steeped in the vices which that situation generates." When, in 1837, Emerson sought a logical antipode for the "American" scholar, he found it in "the courtly muses of Europe." Nearly fifty years later Henry Adams explained that in writing his history of the administrations of Jefferson and Madison he did not intend to give interest "to the society of America itself, but to try for it by way of contrast with the artificial society of Europe."

This handy antithesis of "Europe" has fed our

vague concept of "Americanism." The crudeness of each term is supposedly compensated by the sharpness of the other. In "Europe" we have mentally homogenized the varied cultures of a broad continent. To be sure, the specific family memory which many Americans have possessed of an Irish, Italian, German, or Polish-Jewish habitat has deeply affected their image both of Europe and of America. At different periods and in several parts of the United States (especially on the Pacific coast and in the South) non-European nations have entered our thinking about ourselves. But all these variants have been transient, local, and insignificant compared with our tendency to discover ourselves as a kind of non-Europe.

A host of peculiarities of our history and geography have contributed to our simplistic way of thinking. We have been almost continuously at peace with our nearest neighbors; these near neighbors have never been world powers to whom we wished to compare ourselves. Since the great stream of our settlement has come from Europe, the neat symmetry of origin and destination, point of departure and point of arrival has reinforced the polarity of Europe and America.

The Breakdown of the Polarity of America and Europe: 1914-1945

In several ways, however, the facts of life in the first half of the twentieth century have sowed doubts of this old-fashioned antithesis and have revealed that Americans share the predicament of their fellow men across the Atlantic. Among the most important factors have been the disappearance of the frontier and of "free" land, and the decline of immigration. But these were comparatively gradual and so were not forcibly impressed on the public mind. Other events which assimilated the life of *homo Americanus* to that of *homo Europaeus* were more dramatic. The catastrophes which announced with a deafening roar the convergence of life on the two continents were, of course, the First World War, the Great Depression of 1929, and the Second World War.

Still there was no growing or continuous stream of thought which attempted to reorient the American self-image to our growing assimilation to the conditions of the Old World. But as "citizens of the world" many Americans came to realize that they would have to be concerned with the government of the world. Woodrow Wilson was a prophet, proclaiming a new role for America. In his second Inaugural Address (March 5, 1917) even before American entry into the war, Wilson declared: "The greatest things that remain to be done must be done with the whole world for stage and in cooperation with the wide and universal forces of mankind, and we are making our spirits ready for those things. . . . We are provincials no longer. The tragical events of the thirty months of vital turmoil through which we have just passed have made us citizens of the world. There can be no turning back." He began to speak of "American" principles as "not the principles of a province or of a single continent. We have known and boasted all along that they were the principles of a liberated mankind." The universalistic temper of his utterances deepened with the passage of time. Before the war was over his words had the crystalline brightness of a gospel. Once policy had been elevated into gospel, all the world could be reproached for not accepting it.

During the nineteenth century the American, insofar as he had thought of the question at all, had considered himself a happy deviant from an ancient European norm. But Wilson's Fourteen Points and his program of peace made the United States of America the model for a new Europe. The countries of the Old World were to give up their secret diplomacy, abandon "the great game, now forever discredited, of the balance of power," become self-governing, self-determining states. Beneath all lay the arrogant expectation that through a League of Nations the peoples of France, Germany, Italy, and of many lesser nations would seize the opportunity to deal with each other in the manner of Massachusetts, New York, and California. Wilson's program was not merely an embodied idealism, it was a projection of the American image onto Europe. Many of our historians have shared the Wilsonian illusions. Therefore many of them have written the history of the Peace as if there was something perverse in the unwillingness of the Senate and the American people to go along with Wilson's program for Europe. In the long perspective of our history what is surprising is the opposite: that even a considerable minority of Americans were ready to give up their traditional image of Europe and to begin to think of it as a potential America.

The World War and its European aftermath did not discourage Americans from their vision of a Europe where dissension, misery, and oppression were endemic—a natural antithesis to America. Senator Borah summed up the view of many Ameri-

cans when he noted, in 1934, that history had produced "the same things in crowded Europe for a
thousand years. . . . It has not mellowed the individuality of nations or fostered and strengthened
the spirit of co-operation."

The calm of American political life in the Age of
Coolidge was all the more conspicuous against the
contrast of Europe with its partisan recrimination,
its shifting party alignments, its revolutions and
near-revolutions. Will Rogers in 1926 sketched the
American caricature of Old World politics:

> I arrived in Paris late at night. The next day we had
> Briand Premier for breakfast; Herriot Premier for
> Lunch; Poincaré for Dinner; and woke up the next
> morning and Briand is back in again. This is not a
> Government; it's an old-fashioned Movie, where they
> flash on the screen: "Two minutes, please, while we
> change Premiers." I have had a date to interview every
> one of them, but they were thrown out before the
> Interview time come due.

To this disgust with the apparently senseless dis-
order of European life—documented by a host of
war and postwar novels—was added the specifically
American experience of the War Debts. The perverse "refusal" of the European countries to "pay
back" seemed pure dishonesty: of course, they
didn't do business like us.

In place of passive acceptance of the deep differences between America and Europe, there were new
feelings of resentment and active antagonism. From
our charity we saw ourselves reaping ingratitude
and hatred. Americans were doubly bewildered to
be blamed for the virtues which had made them
the banker, the arsenal—and the Uncle Shylock—
of Europe. Formerly they had felt merely alien to

Europe. Now they felt rejected by a Europe for whose reform they had spent their blood and treasure. Many saw no escape but in withdrawal. So grew a new and articulate isolationism, reaffirming the old polarity with new zest and bitterness.

The Russian Revolutions of 1917 complicated our thinking about Europe. Many Americans (generally not the educated or sophisticated) viewed the overthrow of the Czarist regime as simply another example of the incomprehensible confusion and turbulence of Europe—comparable to the overthrow of a ministry in France or a Balkan *coup d'état*. Some, however, did see a menace in bolshevism. But what they saw was vague and shadowy, like the "Romanism" which had frightened earlier generations or William Randolph Hearst's "Yellow Peril." They lumped bolshevism with anarchism, syndicalism, socialism, free love, atheism, and other unfamiliar notions into a single explosive parcel supposed to have been recently imported from Europe. The infamous raids of Attorney General A. Mitchell Palmer, purporting to seek out dangerous aliens, resulted in the deportation of a few hundred in 1919-20. The new immigration policy, embodied in a series of novel acts beginning in 1917, sought, in Wilson's words, to close "the gates of asylum which have always been open to those who could find nowhere else the right and opportunity of constitutional agitation for what they conceived to be the natural and inalienable rights of men." The crude but traditional American image of Europe as a center of misery, poverty, oppression, aristocracy, and decadence was now tinged by the Russian Revolution with the horrendous red of revolution and anticapitalism. In 1927 Sacco and Vanzetti, two foreigners who happened to be philosophical anarchists, were executed for murder, but were actually scapegoats of a growing fear of all ideas from abroad. The ambivalence of the situation was expressed in the great struggle over that trial, and in the fact that the victims soon entered American folklore as companions of John Brown. We have conveniently forgotten that some patriotic Americans like Edward Bok saw in the Russian Revolution a hope that Russia might in the future prove "a second United States of America."

Wilson's planetary idealism had not convinced many; he expressed the aspirations of only a small minority of his countrymen. But he did voice a sentiment that was bound to grow in an increasingly powerful America. Once we had fought the war and spent American lives and money in Europe it was embarrassing for either political party to argue that we might better have stayed out. It would never again be so easy to believe that America and Europe were incommensurable. Wilson's demand that the world be made safe for democracy expressed the nascent American belief that America should become the norm for the world.

The Literati and the European Cultural Standard for America: The Antithetic Mood

After 1914 vigorous American writers were developing a new framework of national self-criticism. Some of those who showed the greatest gusto in criticizing crude American attitudes unwittingly revealed their domination by the simple-minded American antithesis of Europe versus America. Now, when many things seemed wrong with America, it was seductively easy to invert the old polarity by assuming that what America lacked might be found in Europe, or might be replenished from Europe.

In the eloquent speech which Sinclair Lewis (who in 1926 had refused the American Pulitzer Prize) delivered on the occasion of his acceptance of the Nobel Prize on December 12, 1930, he expressed both the old polarity and the new breakdown of it. There was something very familiar—almost banal— about his observation that "in the new and vital and experimental land of America, one would expect the teachers of literature to be less monastic, more human, than in the traditional shadows of old Europe." But, he remarked, America had not fulfilled the possibilities of this antithesis. The Cambridge-Concord group of the mid-nineteenth century he saw as "sentimental reflections of Europe," who had left no school and no influence. The more recent "New Humanists"—the school of Irving Babbitt and Paul Elmer More—seemed to Lewis but another attempt to make American literature a pallid reflection of European culture.

Clearly, then, in Lewis's opinion, America had not lived up to its opportunity to be a non-Europe. But his proof of this was that we had not produced authors to meet the standard of Europe, that, in his words, we had never had a Brandes, a Taine, a Goethe, or a Croce.

In Sinclair Lewis's own vigorous gropings for a new concept of American literature we discern the common confusion bred by the simple-minded notion that somehow denial of a decrepit Europe would be an affirmation of a young America. Lewis, like many of his fellow writers of the age, still was at a loss to discover a positive content. Thus, he was pleased that we were "coming out of the stuffiness of safe, sane, and incredibly dull provincialism"—that there were new writers with a "determination to give to the America that has mountains and endless prairies, enormous cities and lost far cabins, billions of money and tons of faith, to an America that is as strange as Russia and as complex as China, a literature worthy of her vastness." Lewis was determined to be American: he argued for a literature strenuously American. But he seemed to believe that the drabness and respectability which cursed American life and literature could somehow be refreshed by the waters which ran along the left bank of the Seine. He expressed this obliquely in the Max Gottlieb of *Arrowsmith* (1925), the Dr. Bruno Zechlin of *Elmer Gantry* (1927), and the romanticizing of European life in *Dodsworth* (1929).

The oblique appeal to Europe as the standard by which America was to be judged is nowhere plainer than in H. L. Mencken, the *enfant terrible* of the two decades after 1914. Much of what Mencken was to find laughable in American life is what would have been picked out by a cultivated European aristocrat. But Mencken's method did not encourage or even allow him to make his standards explicit. Many Americans at the time were pleased to think that Mencken was comparing America as it was with America as it ought to be or might be. But as we read him in retrospect it is hard not to notice that the vices, large and small, which irked him in American life were, almost without exception, peculiarly *American* shortcomings, from which Europe had been and would likely remain happily exempt. When he writes of *homo boobiens,* as in his *Notes on Democracy* (1926), he professes to be trying to describe the mobocracy of all times and places; but when we look closely we see that he has, wittingly or unwittingly, drawn an extremely individualized portrait of *homo Americanus.* It is often forgotten that his starting point was Nietzsche, about whom he wrote a book in 1908. Insofar as he had a philosophical base for his writing he had found it in this characteristically European philosopher. And his writings are a miscellany of raucous laughter at peculiarly American institutions.

The kind of satisfaction which the institutional critics drew from attacking their George F. Babbitts and Elmer Gantrys and the other representatives of "boobocracy," was found by the literary critics in their attacks on Longfellow and Lowell and other symbols of American literary timidity. Among the most influential of these was Van Wyck Brooks. His books, too, revealed the dominance of the Old European-American polarity, and the extent to which American thinkers leaned on the very antithesis that they were trying to destroy.

In *America's Coming-of-Age* (1915), Brooks deplored the dualism in an American culture which consisted of "highbrows" at one end and "lowbrows" at the other, and which had produced the pallor of Irving, Cooper, Bryant, and Longfellow in place of the robustness of Darwin, Mill, Carlyle, Newman, Ruskin, Mazzini, and Nietzsche. Having set out to discover the character and conditions of a distinctively American literature, he concluded by measuring American literature and reproaching it by the traditional standard of Europe. His highest praise for Whitman, his lone symbol of a unified

American culture, is that "he would have been perfectly at home in the company of Achilles, or Erasmus, or Louis XIV."

In applying his critical thesis, Brooks showed a singular insensitivity to characteristically American writers like Mark Twain. So antipathetic and incomprehensible did he find the work of this writer out of the West that he was driven, in *The Ordeal of Mark Twain* (1920), to construct an elaborate argument from fragments of psychoanalysis and other evidence. Brooks tortured himself with the necessity of explaining how so talented a writer as Mark Twain could have been diverted from profound and savage satire—supposedly on the Rabelaisian or Swiftian model—into those pleasantries which amused millions of his fellow Americans. In *The Pilgrimage of Henry James* (1925), Brooks revealed that his alternative to the escape into "respectability" which was presumably Mark Twain's solution," was an escape to Europe itself, which was Henry James's "solution."

This way of thought produced what might be called the "antithetic mood" of American critical self-consciousness in the twenties and thirties. The old crude polarity of America versus Europe was serving the more sophisticated thinkers with a framework for their scrutiny of America. They sought to refresh a desiccated America from the European wellspring. When Matthew Josephson wrote his *Portrait of the Artist as American* (1930), he chose for his motto Melville's phrase, "I feel I am an exile here." They nourished the impossible hope that Europe might be reborn in America. At the same time the view of Josephson, Brooks, and others, that there had been an exodus of the American artist from a less congenial American habitat to a much more congenial European one, carried with it the suspicion that the European destination was an artist's Promised Land.

A small, not very influential, but highly articulate group of intellectuals gave extreme expression to the antithesis. A number of critics and philosophers of whom Irving Babbitt and Paul Elmer More were to be the best known, expounded the New Humanism. These writers both distrusted what was characteristically American—seeing our culture embodied in the caricatures of P. T. Barnum and Henry Ford —and uncritically accepted what was most un-American in European culture. More outspokenly than Lewis or Mencken, the New Humanists found the great literary works of European culture and the characteristic attitudes of European aristocracy the proper antidote to the Philistinism of America. "It is doubtful," Norman Foerster observed in *Humanism and America* (1930), "whether a *real* American culture could ever spring from our own experience; it is certain that it could be *caused* to spring from our own experience by a happy use of foreign culture." A later expression of this same attitude was the educational movement of which Mortimer J. Adler and Robert M. Hutchins, former Chancellor of the University of Chicago, were leaders. In their attack on the illiteracy of the American educated classes they tended to redefine the higher learning as the body of European literature; and to redefine the role of education as the preparation of more and more Americans to converse with the cultured men of Europe.

Among the transmutations of the old polarity none was more paradoxical than the growing tend-

ency in the twenties and thirties to see America as
decadent and to find robustness and earthiness in
Europe. By a kind of historical legerdemain, the
roles of America and Europe were reversed. In 1914,
H. L. Mencken, George Jean Nathan, and Willard
Huntington Wright had written a little book, *Europe after 8:15*, in which they contrasted the American businessman preoccupied with newspapers, golf,
and baseball with the warmth, the love, the adventure, and the passion of "Europe"—the country
which they saw of an evening in the bars and cafés
of Vienna, Munich, Berlin, London, and Paris.
Ernest Hemingway, in his *The Sun Also Rises*
(1926) and *Death in the Afternoon* (1932) had begun to find the lessons of life and love and death
(not in the United States but in Italy, Spain, or
Africa) in what had to earlier generations seemed
hardly more than the "brutalities" of backward
cultures.

The old antithesis now seemed neither so simple
nor so vivid as it once had been. We began to find
ourselves confronted by a task of positive definition.
Now we had to discover our relation not merely
to our "roots" but to the whole earth.

The Europeanization of American Political Life: The Antithesis Confused

It was precisely this need to construct an affirmative conception of America that stirred American
self-doubt in the first half of the twentieth century.
The facts of life began to make their impression.
And the profoundest problems of American self-definition between the Great Depression of 1929
and the end of the Second World War arose from
the obvious ways in which we now seemed to share

the ills of Europe. There crept over us the sense that somehow we had been cheated of our uniqueness. We felt the bewilderment of the woman who has been seduced, who feels that it must have been partly her own fault but still is not sure how much.

During the presidential campaign of 1928, Herbert Hoover developed his classic contrast "between the American system of rugged individualism and a European philosophy of diametrically opposed doctrines—doctrines of paternalism and state socialism." Integral with Hoover's contrast was the thesis that the Great Depression had had its large and primary causes in Europe. This thesis (which Hoover later developed with some bitterness in his memoirs) is amply expressed in Hoover's statements between 1928 and 1932. The American economy, he argued, had all the while been fundamentally sound. "Our domestic difficulties standing alone would have produced no more than the usual type of economic readjustment which had re-occurred at intervals in our history." The Depression, in the form of an economic catastrophe rather than a mere business slump, was "an economic hurricane from abroad." From this point of view the Depression was only another lesson (like the First World War) in the importance of the antithesis of America and Europe. And of the Nemesis sure to follow any breach in the wall between the two worlds.

President Franklin Roosevelt did not see the Depression as a hurricane from abroad. Instead, he found its primary cause in the weaknesses of the American economy, and especially in the inability of purchasing power to keep pace with production. His attitude toward the Depression, with his experimental way of thinking about American life and institutions, was to do a great deal to break down the old antithesis. In eager search for expedients he listened to all comers. John Maynard Keynes, Harold Laski—and even Karl Marx—found an interested ear at the White House. Many new political devices were adopted with a new unconcern for whether they had ever before been used in this country.

The influx into Washington of intellectuals and academics acquainted with the history and institutions of other countries brought the foreign experience into government counsels. It was an unfamiliar phenomenon for a president of the United States to write, as he wrote to Harry Hopkins in 1934 urging "that you make a trip abroad as soon as you can possibly get away and look over the housing and social insurance schemes in England, Germany, Austria and Italy, because I think you might pick up some ideas useful to us in developing our own American plan for security."

In many ways, some intended and some accidental, the New Deal helped assimilate the American to the "European" political experience. In the first place, of course, government was given tasks of initiation and control—through such devices as the National Industrial Recovery Act, the Agricultural Adjustment Act, the Works Progress Administration, the Public Works Administration, the Civilian Conservation Corps, the Securities and Exchange Act, the Tennessee Valley Authority, the National Labor Relations Board, and myriad others. Secondly, the New Deal drew heavily on American university faculties and on the American intelligentsia. The intellectual acquired a role in American political life which was not only unprecedented in our own history but which was (at least from the point of view of the professors themselves) happily like that of their European colleagues.

The American political lexicon began to change. Into it came many expressions more familiar in the vocabulary of Europe: "Socialism," "United Front," "Government Control," "Unemployment Insurance," and "Social Security." Perhaps our political parties, like those of France, ought to "stand for something." People responsible for policy began reaching for a "philosophy" of the New Deal which —however elusive and ill-formed—was a kind of concoction of Keynesian economic doctrine, Marxian historical theory, and Neo-Jeffersonian political ideals. Some began to suggest that our labor unions, traditionally characterized by short-term objectives and lack of ideology, ought now to "mature" by developing an ideology and participating actively in elections. The emergence of the Congress of Industrial Organizations (1935), together with its technique of the sit-down strike, its enlistment of the sympathy and collaboration of newspapermen and teachers, and the growth of a Teacher's Union within the American Federation of Labor—all showed similarities to the European pattern. The Political Action Committee of the C.I.O. put unions into politics in a way not familiar in American history. Even the Communist Party was given hospitality in an American "United Front" consciously formed on a European pattern.

In a number of ways, the Lend-Lease Program, our entry into the Second World War in 1941, and our relations with our allies (especially the Soviet Union) during the war contributed to the breakdown of the old polarity. The disintegration by the New Deal of that antithesis which had lain at the heart of Hoover's thinking about the American system now made it easier to identify our war aims with those of Great Britain and the Soviet Union. From January 1, 1942, it was no longer the Allied powers, but "The United Nations"—nations presumably united in social ideals as well as in war aims.

After the death of President Roosevelt on April 12, 1945, and after the surrender of the Axis powers later that year, American political life remained more Europeanized than ever before. Military conscription continued into peacetime. The many new institutions which had broadened the role of the state in American life were preserved as part of the permanent fabric of our society, first, by President Truman's Fair Deal and then by the assent of the Republican administration which came into power in 1953.

But the effective breakdown of the old antithesis was in institutions rather than in thought. And the old polarity has remained prominent in private discussion and public debate. Since the election of 1932, every Republican presidential candidate has attacked the Democratic Party for betrayal of the American tradition by introducing "alien" and "European" concepts and methods into American government; Democratic candidates have in their turn argued that the methods of the New Deal and the Fair Deal were in fact not "foreign" but truly American. Our way of thinking about ourselves and our images of other nations persist in very much the old pattern.

The Persisting Polarity of American Thought: "There Can Be Only One Enemy"

The deep necessities of American geography, history, and institutions have drawn us into the polar way of thinking about ourselves. The motleyness of our population, the multiplicity of our cultural origin, the variety of our continent-nation, the diversity of our regional economies, and the pragmatic and unideological character of our institutions have induced us to define our national character negatively. The polar framework has thus served our need and our disposition to describe our national character and tradition in elusive, vague, and shifting terms. It has required little precision, and demanded little agreement to assert that we stand for everything that Europe is *not*. The emptiness of the polar concept has had the further advantage of leaving us free to experiment without worrying whether we were violating our definition of our own character.

Recent developments in American thinking about herself, about Europe, and about the world show how fundamental is this simple polar framework. For we find it difficult to believe in the existence of more than one enemy at a time. Our naïveté in this respect has never been more striking than during the Second World War, when we reassured ourselves by declaring that the Soviet Union shared our political ideals and international objectives.

So long as we were oriented toward Europe, with a broad stream of immigration arriving from European shores, and with our political and military involvements primarily European, the antithesis of "Europe" was more or less adequate to the construction of our image of ourselves. But at least since the turn of the century, and especially since 1914, our assimilation to Europe and our belief that our political ideals might be shared by large numbers of people in Europe have been growing. Since Wilson's first administration, but especially since the 1930's, our willingness to learn from European experience and institutions has been increasing; the antithesis of "individualism" against "collectivism" is less apt than it once seemed.

We have come more and more to look toward Asia as well as toward Europe in formulating our diplomatic and military policy. In the Second World War for the first time in our history we sent a large expeditionary force to Asian shores. Americans returned with some notion of Burma, Guam, Japan, and Indochina. The trip which Wendell L. Willkie, Republican presidential candidate in 1940, took around the world, and which produced *One World* (1943), included not one Western European capital, but covered many places in the Near East and the Orient. Most important, since 1917 a world revolutionary movement has been at work, and its significance has been gradually, if crudely, recognized in the United States. The arena of conflict of which Americans are aware has broadened to include the world.

The consequence of these and other facts has not been to make us abandon our familiar way of thinking—our traditional tendency to see the United States of America at one end of the antithesis and an image of all possible evils at the other. It has led us rather to fill the framework with a new content. Whereas formerly we were a non-Europe, now we have become a kind of noncommunism. If throughout most of our history Europe was a handy mirror in which to see what we were not, and hence to help us discover what we were, now communism does us the same service. But as the old polarity in its crudeness has grave perils, so has the new. The naïve view, fostered by Woodrow Wilson—that most of the ills of the world might be remedied if we bridged the antithesis by bringing American federalism, representative government, and open diplomacy to countries unfamiliar with them—led us into blind optimism and a desire to embrace the world. That produced its inevitable consequence, a cynical pessimism and nostalgia to be insulated from the world. What has been lacking is a mature willingness to recognize the world and its ways, with its multiple possibilities of decency.

The new form of the old polarity carries the old dangers. True, it solaces us by simplifying the problem, and making "solutions" more conceivable. But to insist that the world be divided into the two insoluble camps of "communism" and "noncommunism" (or "democracy") is to overlook the possibility of institutions which do not fit into either class. Yet we must recognize just such unfamiliar alternatives if we would adequately describe the needs, aspirations, and feasible institutions of large parts of Asia and even of Western Europe. Belief in this simple opposition is, of course, precisely what the agents of world communism wish, and what will most serve their purpose. Because it impresses on many nations wobbling between the Soviet Union and the United States that if they cannot become democratic and capitalist in the American pattern, the Americans will disavow them and lump them with the forces of communism.

There is a grave and frightening difference between the old naïveté and the new. Today, we are in a position not only to *believe* in an oversimplified polarity, but to polarize the actual world. To tell ourselves that perpetual peace would be in sight if communism were only conquered, and that all nations are either "democratic" or "communist," both expresses and reinforces the oversimplified antithesis. There could be no greater catastrophe for American power and diplomacy than success in imposing that misconception on the world.

The last half century with its discovery that there were many Europes, and that we might be part of one of them, has begun to educate us. It has disintegrated the image of a "Europe" which was a mere foil for our image of ourselves. That process of sophistication must go on if we are to modify the equally simple, but vastly more dangerous, polarity which drives all who do not like us, and who do not wish to be like us, into the image and the camp of The Enemy.

2. THE PLACE OF THOUGHT IN AMERICAN LIFE

No one can study the history of thought in Europe without taking account, at the outset, of two basic facts. First, there is the separation of the thought of the community into two streams: the stream of "high culture"—the thought, art, and vocabulary of the aristocrats, priests, and all members of the privileged and ruling classes; and the stream of "popular culture"—the thought, art, customs, lore, and folkways of the great mass of the people. The gulf is so deep and the separation so wide between the two in most European countries, and has been for most of their history, that the definition of what is being talked about offers no problem to the historian of European thought. He is talking about either the "thinking class" or the "working class." It is a truism that in many periods the aristocracy of France felt a closer fellowship with the aristocrats of Germany than with the peasants of their own country. The folk culture of the English people is at least as remote from that of its aristocratic and educated classes as the culture of England is different from that of France or Italy. When, for example, Sir Leslie Stephen wrote his *History of English Thought in the Eighteenth Century*, it was perfectly obvious that he was writing about the ideas which filled the heads of that small fraction of the English population who were literate, educated and close to the seats of power.

Second—and this feature is closely connected with the first—the history of European thought (by which is usually meant the thought of the only "thinking" people, that is the aristocratic classes) is on the whole reducible to the history of systems and schools of thought. It is the history of "Thomism," "Rationalism," "Transcendentalism," et cetera —terms which to most of the people of those days were as foreign as another language. It is the history of the specialized architecture of philosophies, rather than of the general physiology of thinking. The grander, the more filigreed and intricate a system, supposedly the greater its claim to treatment in the history of thought. Those elegant intellectual chapels built by Thomas Aquinas and Immanuel Kant thus have become the destinations of the historians' pilgrimage. Scholars find them a welcome refuge from the confusion of the market place.

But it is misleading to take these characteristics of European thought as the starting points for an American history. Our society, unlike most other modern nations, has not been marked by the separation into high culture and popular culture; nor has our thinking been dominated by systems and schools. On the contrary, there have been a number of other large and persistent characteristics of the place of thought in American life. There are those which concern the *form* of American intellectual life, and those which concern the *substance* of our way of thinking.

I.

Beginning with the form of our intellectual life, we find two important and apparently contradictory characteristics: first, its unity or homogeneity; and second, its diffuseness.

The Unity of American Culture

From one point of view the history of culture in the most developed European countries in modern times has been rather uniform. For the growth of their liberal institutions has not removed their basic distinction between aristocratic culture and folk culture. What has happened is either that their aristocratic culture has been watered down piecemeal to make it more accessible and more palatable to the half-educated masses, or that a few places have been made available within the aristocracy for more talented and ambitious members of the lower classes ("the career open to talent"). A typical example of the first of these was the translation of the Greek and Latin classics into the vernacular languages, which was one of the major intellectual events of the European Renaissance. An example of the second was the growth of a system of scholarships which brought to Oxford and Cambridge some young men whose wealth and ancestry had not entitled them to that advantage. But the basic fact is that the modern intellectual and cultural life of the European community is still simply a modification and adaptation of the old aristocratic (high) culture to the sporadic demands of members of the rising classes. How little progress has yet been made is illustrated by the fact that throughout Western Europe (where alone true universities remain), with insignificant exceptions, a higher education is still the prerogative of the rich and the well-born; but the student population in American colleges and universities is currently over three million. To say the very least, the culture of modern Europe bears the birthmark of its aristocratic origin: it was made by and for the very few, though it may gradually, in some places and to some extent, have become available to a few more.

American culture is basically different from all this. In this, as in so many other ways, here is something new under the sun. With due allowance for the influence of the European doctrine and example, one must not fail to see the vast importance of the peculiar American situation. For ours is a modern culture which skipped the aristocratic phase. While having the literary and vernacular resources of the European Renaissance and the Reformation behind us, we started our culture with some semblance of wholeness and homogeneity. We have been without that deep bifurcation into high and low, which was the starting point of the national cultures of Western Europe.

The student body of Harvard College in the seventeenth century was probably already more representative of the community at large than the universities of many European countries are today. As Samuel Eliot Morison points out, in the earliest years of the College almost every Harvard student was the child of parents who actually farmed the soil, in addition to whatever else they did, and "it does seem that the College was fairly successful, after 1654, in recruiting boys of scholarly ambition from the plain people of New England." Part of the explanation of this phenomenon is found, for Massachusetts Bay at least, in the extraordinarily high proportion of university graduates to the whole population in those earliest years. But this was only one factor which happened to be important in that part of America. The more universal and characteristically American phenomenon was a homogeneity of thought and culture quite alien to the European experience. This was what Governor Thomas Hutchinson described, in the late eighteenth century, as the fact of "the generality of the colony being very near upon a level."

In Europe the progress of liberal and democratic movements has been measured by the extent to which they have broken down the barriers of the old aristocratic culture; anything which made the language and thought of the aristocracy available to more people was considered progressive. But in America the starting point has been the opposite: the unity of our society has been taken for granted. It is, rather, any failure to make culture available to all the people that has required justification.

While European liberals have tried to put the luxury of a classical education within the reach of members of the underprivileged classes, American democrats have attacked the very idea of a classical education because of its aristocratic overtones. Before the end of the eighteenth century, Benjamin Rush opposed the inclusion of Latin and Greek within the standard curriculum of a liberal education for the simple reason that these languages might be difficult for women to learn; and, he urged, nothing should be part of an American education which was not within the reach of all citizens. From the time of Rush and Jefferson to that of John Dewey, our educators have been primarily interested in what Rush called "the mode of education proper in a Republic." Thus, foreign travel and study in a foreign university, basic to the European aristocratic ideal of culture and congenial to the cosmopolitan and international allegiances of their educated classes, were urged by the arbiters of European culture, at least from the seventeenth century. But in 1798, Benjamin Rush asked (in words with which Jefferson would have agreed) that Americans be educated at home rather than in a foreign country. Only in the New World could the unique republican principles of American life be properly reinforced in the young, and only so could the equality of men and the unity of American culture be encouraged. "I conceive the education of our youth in this country to be particularly necessary in Pennsylvania," he wrote, "while our citizens are composed of the natives of so many different kingdoms in Europe. Our schools of learning, by producing one general, and uniform system of education, will render the mass of the people more homogeneous, and thereby fit them more easily for uniform and peaceable government." This desire for uniformity and homogeneity has had, of course, a profound effect on our conception of higher education, particularly in supporting movements to water it down and flatten its flavor to suit everybody's palate. Thus, a profound truth about our culture lurks in Bliss Perry's facetious suggestion that the ideal of American education could most easily be attained by awarding every American citizen the degree of bachelor of arts at birth. There is no denying that we started with the assumption that a society should have a single culture whose highest thoughts should be accessible to most men.

Even our geographic vastness and variety have contributed to this. Because differences of region and climate are so overwhelming, the differences of social classes in the several parts of the country have actually seemed less important. The American who goes to England, France, or Italy cannot but note linguistic versatility as a mark of social caste; the upper classes not only speak their national language with an aristocratic accent, they actually speak several languages. In contrast to this, in the United States, of course, accent is a sign not of class but of regional origin. Even the regional dialects have been much less marked here than in other countries of comparable size. English travelers and American lexicographers noted this in the eighteenth and early nineteenth centuries. "It is agreed," John Pickering observed in 1816, "that there is greater uniformity of dialect throughout the United States (in consequence of the frequent removals of people from one part of our country to another) than is to be found throughout England." On the whole, it is the members of our lower classes who tend to know well another language—such as German or Italian or Yiddish—in addition to English. It is partly by losing their cosmopolitan character, by forgetting all languages other than English, that people become homogenized into American culture. In the United States we all try to speak the same language, and only a few know more than one.

Our ideal of equality has carried with it the fact of universal literacy, and in this and other ways has contributed to the ideal of cultural unity. The

Protestant tradition, our lack of ancient institutions, and the absence of a professional class of articulators—a "learned" or "cultured" class—all these have played their part. Unprecedented technological development, taken together with natural wealth, a high standard of living and a domestic mass-market for all kinds of products, has produced a uniformity of standards of consumption and a homogeneity in the particular articles consumed. In America, brand names (with all they imply of universal familiarity with a single product, of homogeneity of product, and of potentially universal consumption of the same product) are symbols of the unity of our culture. A Ford car and a Bendix washer are owned by the chairman of the board of directors as well as by the night watchman. Finally, our yen for orthodoxy has encouraged people both to wish for and to believe in a unity in our ways of thinking and acting.

The Diffuseness of American Intellectual Life

A feature complementary to the aristocratic starting point of European culture is the sharpness with which it is focused on one or a few centers. In modern Europe, the intellectual capital is almost as universal a phenomenon as the aristocracy. Almost every country has had its Paris, its mecca of culture, where one could sit and be at the center of things. One of Europe's main appeals to the American intellectual who has had even a taste of it is the ease with which the focus of intellectual influence and power can be discovered. The young American who goes to Oxford or Cambridge has the comfortable feeling of knowing—or being in a position to get to know—everybody who is anybody in English culture. The other day I talked with a young American student who had just returned from a couple of years in one of the English universities. Having been only another student in America, required to show what he could do in order to acquire a status, he had found himself suddenly offered a position of status and privilege simply because he was a student at Cambridge, England. "It's awfully comfortable," he said, "to be one of the ruling class." After such an experience, the young American cannot but feel a loss of privilege as well as a loss of bearings when, on return to the United States, he discovers that there is no such center.

Only occasionally have we had something like an elite, a group which took to itself the privileges—and claimed the immunities—of the intellectual ruling classes of Europe. The most recent and most striking (and the most difficult for our intellectuals to forget) was the New Deal, when American intellectuals had a taste of that sense of power and of sitting at the center which has been familiar to those of Europe.

Looking at our history as a whole, one sees a diffuseness and a shifting of intellectual life quite alien to the modes of culture in the great nations of Europe. True, different cities have had their days of glory: Boston, Philadelphia, Williamsburg, New York, Chicago, and others. But none has had much more than a day. Our cultural center has been nowhere because it has been everywhere. We are rare among modern nations in having found it necessary and possible to create, *ad hoc,* a special city to serve as the national political capital; that city has never been our cultural capital. The more recent examples of Canberra and New Delhi can probably also be explained by a comparable diffuseness in the cultural life of Australia and of India.

II.

Turning from the form of American intellectual life to the substance of our way of thinking, we find a number of equally striking characteristics. They describe the peculiar vitality and formlessness of our culture. The more rigid and dead the thought of a people, the more easily it is described and reduced to the systems which delight and comfort the academic mind. The more alive a culture and its ways of thought, the more elusive it is and the harder to capture it in systems and categories. The following characteristics are actually ways of describing the elusiveness of American culture.

Interest in Institutions Rather than Ideologies, in Process Rather than Product

Our most important and most representative thinkers have been more interested in institutions than in ideologies. For an ideology is something fixed and rigid: it is a posture of the truth which some men see in one age and which they seek to get other men to accept as the whole truth. But institutions live and grow and change. They have a life of their own as a philosophy cannot; and our major accomplishments have been in the realm of institutions rather than of thought.

At least since the eighteenth century, observers of our society have noted equality as a characteristic of American life. But it is the *fact* rather than the *theory* of equality which has flourished here. If European countries have been strong in theories of equality, as in other political theories, they have been feeble in developing equalitarian institutions. In the United States, on the contrary, where we have had unprecedented success in developing the institution of social equality, we have never been able to produce a pretty or an important theory about it. This is but an example, if one of the more spectacular, of how our talent for improving life has excelled our capacity for perfecting thought.

We have shown very little interest in producing things which would endure: monuments have not been in our line. We have been more concerned with whether an idea or a thing actually serves its purpose than whether it will continue to serve that purpose for a day or a century. We have been anxious not to freeze the categories of thought, for we are ready to believe that old purposes and old needs will be supplanted by new. In exhibiting his plant, an Italian businessman will show with pride the original workshop where his great-great-grand-father started work and which is still in use; an American businessman points out with pride that not a brick of his original plant remains, that the old has been thoroughly replaced by superior modern materials.

Our lack of interest in systems of thought, in ideologies and philosophies, is but a particular illustration of our general lack of interest in perfecting the *product*. This goes with our special interest in improving the *process*. We have been more interested in how and whether things work than in how beautiful they can be in themselves. Our architecture has been concerned less with houses than with housing; our engineers, less with producing sturdy automobiles than with developing satisfactory transportation. We have been interested less in good food than in satisfactory diet. We have been worried less over the content of an education, the meaning of truth, knowledge, and culture, than over understanding and improving the learning process. Our dramatic artists have been less anxious to produce rounded and enduring works of dramatic art than to provide moments and experiences of entertainment and amusement. The "movies"—from this point of view appropriately and significantly named—is the most characteristic of American art forms. It is an artistic object which from its very nature can never be grasped as a whole; the form is elusiveness itself. It cannot be held in the hand and examined for its perfection, like a play of Shakespeare or an oil painting. It can *only* be experienced; and its "meaning" is the accumulated sensation of many separate moments.

About a century ago, Sir Henry Maine made his famous suggestion that "the movement of the progressive societies has hitherto been a movement from Status to Contract." There is a great deal of truth in his observation, even when applied to American as contrasted with European society. But a more general principle, of which Maine's maxim is in this case but a corollary, is that the transit of civilization from Europe to America has been a movement from product to process, from art to institutions, from an interest in things to an interest in ways. The great wealth of America has actually had much to do with this. The abundance of our material resources has encouraged a wholesome unconcern for material things in themselves. We have been able to afford to experiment with the ways of doing a job without worrying about preserving any of the particular physical devices perfected for the purpose. If they no longer do, we throw them away and try others. Thus, our domestic architecture, unlike that of Europe, is not the production of inheritable estates, but the perfection of housing; our automobiles are not heirlooms (as they have become in England or in Italy), but transportation; our dress manufacturers, instead of producing garments which are beautiful and durable, aim to offer the wearer the sensation of being modish for a season.

Never has a people been more wasteful of the things of the earth, and never has that waste expressed greater contempt for the things of this world. America and Asia, as W. H. Auden observes, have in common the fact that they are built on waste: Asia on the waste of human life, America on the waste of material wealth. While scarcity has tempted people in Europe to treat physical means as if they were ends, to give them the reverence and the loving care which the objects of this world may not deserve, the people of the United States have tended to treat all means as expendable and have become preoccupied with getting the job done. In the secondhand-automobile market in Turin, Italy, when I went to sell a car which I had used for a year, the dealers felt its pulse, listened to its cough, and pityingly, almost tenderly, remarked that it was *stanca*—"tired." When in Chicago I took my used car to such a market, the dealer looked hastily at his handbook, rather than the car, told me what a machine of that vintage was worth, and turned quickly to persuade me of the superior operating advantages of a new model. The printed word, in the form in which it reaches most people here, aims less to be a rounded literary product than a means of entertainment, of topical and relevant instruction, of information on the qualities and prices of all the other available means of living.

In this sense—contrary to current clichés about us—our willingness to waste things has expressed our unconcern for the things of life and our greater interest in the ways of life. Our distinctive interest in process has been expressed in myriad aspects of American culture which have enabled us to see through the object to the objective; to view art not as the perfection of artistic objects, but as a kind of experience; to see religiosity not in the construction of religious monuments and churches, but in a "religious experience" for which the church building is only an instrument.

In the realm of material things, all this has been encouraged basically by our great material wealth with all it has meant in the way of an indefinitely expandable market and a continuing demand for better ways of doing all sorts of things. The distinction here is crucial. For example, we must not consider the growing demand for air conditioners in middle-class homes as a simple expression of materialism and greed for more things of this world. It is more precise to recognize this as but another illustration of our passionate preference for the experience of being cool in summer and for being comfortable in many other ways.

In the realm of ideas, this frame of mind has carried a distinctive lack of interest in the form of thought, a cavalier indifference to whether our thought is consistent and systematic. We are immensely interested in ideas when they wear work clothes, when they are embodied in ways of life. We

are less interested in how they sound in the salon
or from the lecture platform than in how they
function in the market place.

The Success Criterion

The intellectual landscape of contemporary
Europe is haunted by the ghosts of lost causes.
There is hardly a movement in the checkered history of a European nation which does not have its
active partisans today. A catalogue of living philosophies in Italy now is an index to Italian history.
In those more metaphysically minded countries,
which have possessed dominant intellectual classes,
political parties are ideological. Philosophers classify themselves as disciples of dead centuries. And
all intellectual life becomes a museum of past
ideologies. Where ways of thought are judged by
their intellectual consistency and by their aesthetic
appeal, by their appeal to a distinctively intellectual ruling class rather than by their ability to
become embodied in institutions, the intellectual
life of the community becomes one with the specu-
lations of its visionaries and the vagaries of its
metaphysicians. And this is true in most of the
countries of Europe.

But in the United States, almost from the beginning, our ideas have been tested by their ability to
become embodied in institutions. Puritanism was
to prove itself in Zion; Quakerism in a City of
Brotherly Love. Where success is a test of truth,
men lost interest in lost causes. They cannot be
excited by ideas or philosophic systems (however
symmetrical or well constructed or well argued)
which do not still give promise of being put into
practice. The feasibility of a philosophy becomes

one with its validity. The intellectual vision of the community becomes confined by the limits of the practical. This may bound the speculative life, but it has its advantages.

Defeat and oblivion become a single fate. Somehow, systems of thought seem to lose their immortality; if only once proved unworkable, they die. Thus, intellectual life in the United States at any moment is both more and less cumulative than elsewhere. For our history is a process of elimination which has disposed of irrelevant ideas; and the living ideas at any particular time are all those remaining ideas with some reasonable prospect of adoption. If our intellectual life is a less rich museum for philosophers, it may be a richer tool house for cultivating our garden.

The Importance of Context: The Implicitness of Ideas

Never before was a culture so much nourished on the belief that values grow from the context, that the appropriate way of thinking grows out of the particular style of living: "We ever held it certain," declared Cabeza de Vaca in 1535, "that going toward the sunset we would find what we desired." The Puritans, too, believed that Westward the course of the Gospel would have its way: following Jesus' prophecy in Matthew 24:27, they were confident that, as the light of the Gospel had formerly shone out of the East, so now it would shine out of the West. Through the eighteenth and nineteenth centuries—from Crèvecoeur's notion that America had produced a new man, through Jefferson's belief in the wealth, promise, and magnificence of the continent, and Turner's

faith in a frontier-born culture and frontier-nour-
ished institutions—runs the refrain that American
values spring from the circumstances of the New
World, that these are the secret of the "American
Way of Life." This refrain has been both an
example of our special way of dealing with ideas
and an encouragement to it. For lack of a better
word, we may call this a leaning toward *implicitness,* a tendency to leave ideas embodied in experience and a belief that the truth somehow arises
out of the experience.

This carries with it a preference for the relevance
of ideas as against their form and a surprising unconcern for the separability of ideas. We have
seldom believed that the validity of an idea was
tested by its capacity for being expressed in words.
The beliefs that values come out of the context
and that truth is part of the matrix of experience
(and hardly separable from it) become themselves
part of the way of American thinking—hence, the
formlessness of American thought, its lack of
treatises, schools, and systems.

The Nirvana of Success: Self-annihilation through Mastery and Adaptation

All this has produced a quaint inversion of the
Buddhist approach to life, or rather something like
an American notion of Nirvana. For the Buddhist,
bliss is attained by the loss of personal identity, by
being absorbed into the universal oneness and
nothingness. His self-annihilation is arrived at by
transcending the physical environment, by rising
above wind and rain, hunger, life and death. The
characteristic notion of bliss developed on the
American continent involves a comparable process

of absorption and loss of identity. But here that oneness is attained by a complete adaptation to the environment which involves seizing the opportunities which it offers, by "fitting in." The objective is an almost mystic and naïvely sensed accord with everything about one. The oblivion of Nirvana and the oblivion of success have much in common. In both, the individual transcends his own personality to become part of what surrounds him. The desire to master the forces of nature, to wrest from the environment all the wealth it holds, to find all possible uses of every material—this has carried with it a willingness to adapt to the social situation, to make the social norm not the fulfillment of some preconceived, philosophy-sharpened ideal, but the fulfillment of the possibilities in the situation, the attainment of compromise. So, for the American, it is not Nirvana, but Rotariana.

Continuity and Conservatism of Ways of Thought

Perhaps never before has there been a society with such remarkable continuity in its ways of thought from the time of its first settlement. The success criterion, the implicitness, the concern for institutions—all these have prevented abrupt breaks in the direction of our thought. For the chain of circumstances is not casually broken as the chain of ideas can be. A philosopher in his study can think up a new and sometimes attractive frame of ideas; he can propose an anarchy, a revolution, or a new beginning; he is free as the air. But circumstances hold within them certain limits; every event somehow grows out of its predecessors. And American empiricism has tied our thinking to the slow, organic growth of institutions. By rejecting ideologies, we reject the sharp angles, the sudden turns, the steep up-and-down grades, which mark political life in many parts of the world, in favor of the slow curves, the imperceptible slopes of institutional life. If ever the circumstances of a culture have suited a people to think "institutionally," American history has done so. For us, fortunately, it is impossible to distinguish the history of our thought from the history of our institutions.

3. THE MYTH OF AN AMERICAN ENLIGHTENMENT

One of the most respectable stereotypes which gets in the way of our seeing the American experience is the notion of the "Enlightenment"—a light which dawned in Europe in the later seventeenth century and which supposedly dazzled the New as well as the Old World at least until the early nineteenth century. The notion that that was an "Enlightened Age" especially appeals to us, of course, because those were the years when our nation was born. It is flattering to think that we were born in the bright light of Reason. It is also academically very convenient: we can then grasp the thought of our philosophically inarticulate Founding Fathers by simply letting the European *philosophes* speak for them.

So many of our best historians have so long taken all this for granted that it may at first seem like arguing that Bacon wrote Shakespeare to propose now that the American "Enlightenment" is largely a myth. Yet if we look closely at the facts—keeping our eyes as much as possible on facts about America —they may suggest that the stereotype is itself a kind of Baconian hypothesis. And that to deny that a European Enlightenment authored American thinking in the eighteenth century is simply to say, after all, that Shakespeare himself wrote Shakespeare. I am arguing for the obvious, which has been obscured by venerable academic clichés.

The notion of an American Enlightenment may best be described as a set of highly sophisticated oversimplifications. To try to dissolve them and to recapture our naïveté will lead us beyond the eighteenth century. For such oversimplifications are precisely the devices by which the rising social sciences have deprived the historian of his traditional vocation as the high priest of uniqueness.

If the historian has any function in the present welter of the social scientific world, it is to note the rich particularity of experience, to search for the piquant aroma of life. As contrasted with the abstract, antiseptic dullness of numbers, "cases," and prototypes. The historian as humanist is a votary of the unrepeatability of all experience, as well as of the universal significance of each human life. Of course the unique cannot be seen as unique except by reference to a universal (and the word "unique" is itself such a one), yet there are important practical differences of emphasis. Today the historian is qualified for a kind of emphasis on individuality which is too rare in our world. Social scientists are preoccupied with what could be called the "modal" approach; they are dominated by the statistical notion of "the category, value, or interval of the variable having the greatest frequency." They focus on such concepts as "status," "personality types," and "occupational mobility" which transcend time and place. And historians who boast of having become interdisciplinary are often only confessing that they no longer burn any tapers before the altar of human uniqueness.

Our greatest historians—whatever else they may have done—have somehow added to our understanding of precisely what it meant to be alive in a particular time and place in the past. Today especially it is important that the historian preserve the ancient naïve assumption that in many ways the experience of different times and places, and of different men and women, are *not* commensurable with each other.

But we all suffer powerful temptations to homogenize experience, to empty each age of its vintage flavor in order to provide ever larger receptacles into which we can pour an insipid liquor of our own making. By homogenizing I mean the tendency to make ideas or things seem more alike in order to serve some current purpose. There are two large classes of homogenizing: the chronological (or vertical), which forcibly assimilates the experience of different periods in the past; and the spatial (or horizontal), which assimilates the experience of different places in the same period. And there are, of course, combinations of the two.

Temptations multiply when we speak about our early national past: for *ex hypothesi* we find there a "seedtime" of the national spirit. In almost all periods of our history it has seemed an act of national piety to homogenize the whole American past; this has done greatest violence to the earlier period. George Bancroft praised the Pilgrims because they were "never betrayed into the excesses of religious persecution," and the founders of Massachusetts Bay for the "mildness and impartiality" of their civil government; similarly Vernon L. Parrington saw Roger Williams as "a forerunner of Locke and the natural-rights school, one of the notable democratic thinkers that the English race has produced," and Jefferson as an "Agrarian Democrat." Related to this is the tendency to homogenize individual men, by using a "great" man an unwitting spokesman for other men in his own or later ages. Thus Franklin is made the apotheosis of the average colonial American of his day, or "The First Civilized American"; Patrick Henry the voice of the Revolution; Jefferson the pre-embodiment of later liberals.

Some kinds of homogenizing come from the pedagogic temptation to paste together fragments of the past to make a subject matter more coherent, more teachable, more discussable, or more write-about-able. For example, among historians of the Protestant churches in America, we find (in a writer like W. W. Sweet) that the American Revolution is closely identified with evangelical, humanitarian, and revivalist movements, and is assumed to be a revolt against things British; this leads to the assumption that the Anglican Church was essentially a British institution (even in America), and hence that Anglicanism must on the whole have nourished Loyalism. Such historians then insist on the anti-Revolutionary tendencies within Anglicanism, and so overlook much of the novelty of Virginia Anglicanism, which was actually a kind of school in self-government.

Or there is the tendency of the cosmopolitan historian. As the patriotic, the vertical (or chronological) homogenizer makes Roger Williams or Thomas Jefferson a herald of movements which he never knew and to which he would have felt alien, or Alexander Hamilton an eighteenth-century version of a twentieth-century capitalist, so the cosmopolitan historian puts the particular thinker into a larger context than that of which he was actually aware. What one does by overlooking the importance of time, the other does by overlooking the importance of space. Of the cosmopolitan historian we find two diverse examples in Carl Becker and Irving Babbitt. In his little book on the Declaration of Independence, Carl Becker describes (under the heading "The Natural Rights Philosophy") certain ideas found in books in England and France in the eighteenth century; then, with very little proof, he suggests that these ideas must have been in American heads. The Enlightenment is hypothesized as a world-wide movement, a "climate of opinion" which everybody inhabited. In the writings of Irving Babbitt, we find the same type of cosmopolitan homogenizing: but for him Jefferson is the American mouthpiece of Anglo-French Romanticism and its French Antichrist, Rousseau. Still another type of homogenizing, which requires less illustration, is that encouraged by the growth of social science, which searches for its own kind of stereotypes, whether they be the "colonial" phenomenon, seen in the writings of Charles M. Andrews, or the phenomenon of "revolution," for example, in Crane Brinton's *Anatomy of Revolution.*

A decisive pressure to homogenize—though one which we can perhaps do least about—comes from the very passage of time. The destruction of records, and the perverting knowledge of how the story actually ended, seem to simplify the raw data of life in every past age. Thus my friends in the Oriental Institute seem able to see so many more general features of life in ancient Egypt or Mesopotamia than we can see in the American eighteenth century.

All homogenizing inevitably deprives the ways of eighteenth-century Americans of their uniqueness in order to instruct us in something supposedly more interesting or significant: the American national destiny, the liberal tradition, the American church, the world-climate of opinion, or the general anatomies of empires and revolutions. Every such emphasis tempts us to overlook some commonplace possibilities about their actual ways of thought. Let me suggest a few.

The Eighteenth-Century Mind as a Miscellany and a Museum vs. the Logical Construct of Historians

Alongside the romantic belief that there were Giants in the Earth in days gone by, must be placed the myth that there were Philosophers in the Earth. Nothing is more misleading (or more unjustified by the facts) than the assumption that the mental furniture of living men at any particular period in the past possessed a logical or stylistic unity. For thought, like experience, is cumulative. We know from introspection that twentieth-century thinking is a mélange of contradictory elements, and of relics from many periods. Yet we somehow expect from eighteenth-century thinking a coherence which would have been possible only if the world had been created anew in the year 1700, and if men had been more insistent logicians than they have ever wanted to be or were capable of being.

For us historians it is especially tempting to assume this logical consistency in the mind of past ages: we can then extrapolate our limited knowledge about the past into the vast realms of our ignorance. How convenient if because Jefferson told us that he believed A, he must also have believed the logical consequences of A! But in my own reading, I have found this assumption misleading. It is a mistake to think that because Jefferson expressed "deistical" sentiments, he was necessarily not also a good Christian or Anglican; that because he believed in "representative" government, he must not have believed in any logically contradictory form of aristocracy. Our intellectual historians seem to me often simply documenting a supposed logical or aesthetic coherence rather than seeking the peculiar incoherence that may have characterized the thinking of an age. Logical consistency within individual books has, of course, nothing to do with the case: we are not books and neither were the men of the eighteenth century. What men do with their ideas is often the only clue to their thoughts; if they acted inconsistently, why must we assume that they thought with consistency? May it not be more useful to discover the circumstances under which many eighteenth-century Virginians found it actually possible to be both deists and Anglicans, republicans and aristocrats? Many of us are confronted with analogous problems. May we not learn as much from the inchoate idea, the pregnant chaos, or the peculiar inarticulateness of a past age, as from its treatises?

The Provincialism of Eighteenth-Century Americans vs. the Cosmopolitanism of Twentieth-Century American Scholars

I have become increasingly impressed with how much more Irving Babbitt and Carl Becker knew about English and French thought of the eighteenth century than was known by Franklin or Jefferson or Washington or Madison. It is so easy for the scholar after the fact, sitting in a vast library, to take in the world at his view, to envisage England, France, and Colonial America at a single glance, that he is understandably tempted to imagine that the colonial American must have been living in that same broad world. But even a man like Jefferson did not in fact live in what we have been taught to call "The World of the Eighteenth Century," or "The Age of the Enlightenment." Paradoxically, he spent by far the greater and more significant part of his life in Virginia. How much of his thought arose from, or was indelibly flavored by, the peculiarities of his situation, rather than from all-pervading grand principles supposedly "in the air" all over the world?

A few of our best scholars, like Carl Bridenbaugh, Julian Boyd, Louis B. Wright, Thomas Jefferson Wertenbaker, Frank Luther Mott, Clarence S. Brigham, Lawrence C. Wroth, Dumas Malone, Douglas Freeman, George MacLaren Brydon (all drawing on the works of earlier scholars like Philip Alexander Bruce), and others have enriched our knowledge of the vivid particularity of that Virginia life. But our vested belief as intellectual historians in that miasma—"The Enlightenment"—still hides from us the actual landscape and mindscape of many parts of the earth. Did not the peculiarities of Jefferson's situation on a Virginia plantation filter all books and ideas from England and France? The machinery by which Jefferson and his fellow Virginians selected those books and ideas was, of course, a decisive feature of their society and their thinking.

Still pedagogical, logical, and aesthetic temptations overwhelm us. How much less troublesome it is to treat eighteenth-century Virginians as an illustration of an omnipresence called "The Eighteenth-Century Mind"—which had no local habitation because it lived everywhere and nowhere—than to start with the opposite assumption that then (as now) the world looked very different from different vantage points.

Social history is a tantalizing miscellaneous subject. But are we justified in assuming that intellectual history is its happy opposite? What seems more irrelevant to the great issues of philosophy than the soil of Virginia, its population, climate, the price of its labor, the cost of its tobacco, the value of its money, the size, circulation, and content of its magazines, and the availability or readability of its books? Why must intellectual history deal in the structure of century-extended, world-encompassing minds, while political history has risen to the level of the specific? Do we not defeat our purpose if we presume "The Eighteenth-Century Mind" somehow different from the thinking of individual men? May we not learn more, even though it be miscellaneous, if we seek the sum of ways of thinking of men in a thousand different places?

The Empiricism of Living Men vs. the Philosophic and Literary Predilections of Intellectual Historians

One of the commonest and most misleading assumptions of intellectual historians is that in a period like the eighteenth century the content of a man's library was roughly the same as the content of his mind. With something of a shock, I have lately realized how little we know about the literacy and actual reading (not book-ownership) of the eighteenth-century Americans. How few Americans of that age are there whose reading we can describe with any confidence! Many literary historians, like Moses Coit Tyler, for example, take the archaeological approach, and in drawing their picture of the eighteenth-century mind give greatest prominence to the most monumental or most aesthetically appealing remains. Many intellectual historians, like Parrington, posit the existence, on purely circumstantial grounds, of a phlogistonlike atmosphere of thought: once an earlier thinker like Locke had been diffused into it, no intellectual combustion could take place into which Locke is not supposed to have entered.

Unmasked there remain some of the very questions which we know, again from common experience, to be crucial to the way living men think. How many of the leading notions held by Jefferson and his Virginia contemporaries may have arisen from common experience in their particular place, rather than from books or the ideas of distant philosophers? Perhaps some of the ideas which have been assumed to be American expressions of the all-pervading Anglo-French Enlightenment actually sprang in some way out of the special Virginia or New World experience? Perhaps that experience was crucial in affecting the ideas to which they were receptive, the books which they not only imported, but actually read? The idea of progress, for example, in the form in which Jefferson and others in the American colonies held it may be less an expression of an historical apriorism, or of the optimism of a French *philosophe,* than a generalization of the spectacular advance of the American colonies during their century. May not the concept of equality (or more precisely of mobility) in the Jeffersonian form (which included strong doubts about the Negro) be less an expression of Rousseauistic egalitarianism than a simple way of describing the actual mobility and opportunity of life in the New World? May not Jefferson's breadth of interest (significantly lacking from many of his eminent urban or New England contemporaries) be less an American translation of French or English encyclopedism than the attempt of an intelligent and experimental plantation-owner to encompass the problems of weather, economy, agronomy, botany, and government forced on him as a plantation-owner and a member of the Virginia aristocracy?

Someone might suggest that this list of consequences of homogenizing the mind of the past ought properly not to be considered a description of the myopia, the willful-believing, or the methodological weaknesses of intellectual historians, but rather as the normal psychology of all historians. Are these homogenized units nothing but the *Gestalten,* the only meaningful, graspable configurations, in which we can organize our data about human thinking in the past? I think not. It is true that if, after staring a long while at the dazzling figure of an Eighteenth-Century Enlightenment, we then turn our eyes suddenly to any novel mass of facts, we do find The Enlightenment impressed as a kind of after-image on the new collection of facts. But, unlike the visual after-image, this is one which we can train ourselves not to see. We can at least refresh our tired vision, to see things which we had never seen before but which we must see if we are to discern the living complexity of eighteenth-century Virginia—or of anyplace else. We will have gained something if only we cease asking of the past questions which it cannot answer, and no longer tantalize ourselves with mirages of beautiful mental oases.

Does this mean, then, that intellectual history must be a form of biography? In the strictest sense, I suppose it does. But may there not also be collective biography, which takes account of the inner tensions and disorders, the limited vision and local needs of groups of particular men in particular places? If instead of solacing ourselves by the way we put the question, if instead of asking what we can learn from the system of thinking which supposedly comprised The Eighteenth-Century Mind, we are frankly enumerative and atomistic, may we not also discover something to our benefit?

Perhaps the greatest service of recent scholarship and of the decisive ways of reorganizing experience which we have learned in the last century has been to offer us new doubts about the academically stereotyped "system" of eighteenth-century thought. Each new framework for interpreting contemporary social experience can help us discover some new realm of ignorance in our understanding of the whole past—including of course the eighteenth century. After Marx, we should never again be so complacent about our understanding of the economic factor in eighteenth-century political life. The Revolution and the Constitution should never again seem so simple; the Whig interpretation will have to meet new and more exacting tests. After Freud, it should never again be so easy to write so confidently about the private life and personal motivation of Washington and Franklin and Jefferson. Since the recent growth of opinion-research we cannot be so facile in our generalizations about "The Colonial Mind" or popular thinking in the Age of the Revolution. These new techniques of interpretation have not themselves provided us with substantive truths about the eighteenth century. But they have helped us discover that there are many more things we do *not* know about the eighteenth century than we had ever suspected.

Thus every overstated insight into the present may providentially open unexplored vistas of our ignorance about the past. The almost overwhelming temptation after every new discovery of a realm of ignorance is, of course, to invent knowledge to fill it up. From Marx there stemmed crude economic interpretations of the American Revolution and the Constitution; and from Freud still cruder psychoanalytic biographies. But are we not better off because Marx and Freud have helped us more sharply define the limits of our past knowledge?

Similarly may not every advance toward understanding the myriad particularity of the thinking of different men in different places in the eighteenth century also help us discover new realms of our ignorance about ourselves? When we use homogenized stereotypes—whether of the American national tradition or of the Enlightenment—to interpret the eighteenth century, we are often doing little more than talking to ourselves about ourselves.

Yet how much could we not discover about ourselves (that we did not even know that we did not know) if we could see ourselves in the journal of any traveler into our twentieth century from eighteenth-century America! We might, for example, begin to discover what we have forgotten while learning the novelties of the last century and a half. By looking through conflict to the epic of progress (as Darwin taught us), by looking beneath reason to rationalization (as Marx and Freud taught us), by seeing ambivalence in every sentiment (as Freud taught us), what have we blinded ourselves to seeing which is on the very surface of experience? Do we no longer admire character because we see only personality? Do we no longer value institutions because we see the ugly motives that have made them? Do we stumble over our own articulateness? We can be sure that we would be asked these, and many other embarrassing questions. And we can also be sure that a Hume, a Gibbon, a Montesquieu, a Voltaire, a Washington, a Franklin, or a Jefferson would each have his particular way of embarrassing us, and of showing us how little we know about ourselves. By describing our past as so much more simple than we know our present to be, have we not deprived ourselves of much of the solace and illumination that the living past has to offer us?

4. AN AMERICAN STYLE IN HISTORICAL MONUMENTS

For nearly every country in Europe, the past is the storehouse of greatness and romance, which declines into the prosaic, insoluble problems of the present. Aristocratic cultures recapture the glories of their history in the crumbling monuments of ancient castles, forts, and palaces. It becomes a patriotic act to leave the remains of that past in their surviving disarray. "There were giants in the earth in those days." Restoration would only cover up the masters' sure touch with the bungling brush strokes of latter-day amateurs. The ruins of the past must be left unrepaired because past magnificence (even in ruins) is more awe-inspiring than the glossy neatness of pigmy moderns. Better a sketch or a fragment by Michelangelo than a completed work done by one of us. In Europe ruins inspire and stimulate the present with confidence in the national genius and an avenging hatred against the barbarian who destroyed the grandeur. They stir unfulfillable yearnings toward the ancient greatness. A ruined Forum is the best propaganda for a Mussolini—and much better than a working model of the Forum would have been: its every scar is a prod to national pride.

In older cultures nearly every monument was built from the half-crumbled ruins of earlier ones. The grand public buildings of the Forum and the Colosseum provided a stone quarry for medieval Christian churches, which were themselves often built on the foundation of pagan temples. Any wholehearted effort to restore the Forum would erase the footsteps of more recent momentous events, in the Middle Ages and the Renaissance. Therefore the typical pathway into the grand European past is the carefully preserved ruin; or the museum (often a defunct palace) crammed full of precious *objets d'art,* sculpture, and painting, which had been produced for a small aristocratic class.

Our American avenues to our past (our counterparts of ruins, museums, and monuments) are very different.

We View the Present as the Climax of History

The unidirectional character of American history—with no lost imperial grandeur in our past —makes us unwilling to abase ourselves before the greatness of any earlier epoch. The great men and the great works of our national history seem great to us precisely because they are still alive. In the national folklore, the Founding Fathers, who fought and compromised for the ideals of religious conscience, political liberty, equality, independence, constitutionalism, and federalism, are great precisely because their ideals live in America today. They cannot stir irredentist movements or nostalgia for a lost empire; in the South we see some glimmering of such hopes, but they are not important, and they are now dying a permanent death. The Federal Constitution is adored because it still works. We view our national history—and the facts justify us—as a single broad stream, the unbroken living current of an American Way of Life, not as a miscellaneous series of great epochs. Partly for this reason we lean more heavily on our past than on our political ideology as a resource for discovering our present, and for defining our ideals. And we have a simpler problem than has the Old World. Our past, unlike theirs, contains fewer contradictions; and we demand that it explain itself to us by giving meaning to our present.

Our Past Has Not Built Monuments for Us

The traveler to Europe or the Orient spends much of his time viewing pyramids, tombs, and palaces: obtruding landmarks in which long-dead men asserted their greatness. All these monuments betray some doubt that the future will remember and understand the past by merely incorporating its ways of life. They express a belief in perfected permanent *things* rather than in persisting, improving *ways*. But there has been no American Ozymandias!

The Democratic Past of a Mobile People Uses Up, Improves, and Replaces Its Artifacts

The remains of past aristocratic cultures (even these which were not constructed on purpose to impress us) are often well preserved because they were so little used. The elegant libraries found all over Europe, with their copies of sixteenth- and seventeenth-century books in mint condition (sometimes with uncut pages), attest to aristocracy more than to literacy. Often books were well preserved simply because they were rarely read and then usually by men of genteel manners. But ours is a culture of newspapers and magazines, which only professors preserve. Often the most widely used books leave the barest trace. The hornbook—the ABC which was in the hand of every New England child—was used up, and perhaps not one remains from the seventeenth century. The New England Primer, the catechism in which children learned at the same time how to read and what to believe, was probably the commonest book in their houses in the seventeenth and eighteenth century; but from the early period we now possess few authentic examples. The inventories of the estates of eighteenth-century Virginians often list "pieces of books"—evidence not of their illiteracy but of their frequent use of books. The bibliophile, the curator of museums of fine arts, and the historian of the most impressive architectural monuments is often polishing the relics of a small aristocracy. But remnants of the widespread ways of life are gone with the wind.

In contrast to all this, the movement of Americans across the face of the continent led them to build only what would do until they could afford better. They hoped to move on and up to better things. Social mobility made most people in most parts of the country glad to tear down the old homestead in order to do better for their children, and to bury their humble ancestry. American technological progress in the nineteenth and twentieth century made the very idea of an heirloom obsolete. Any business that handed its heirs a "museum piece" was preparing for bankruptcy.

Few American parents dream of passing down their house as a family headquarters; instead they hope that each of their children will afford something up to date. In America, except among a precious few, the "antique" is hardly distinguished from the "secondhand."

The self-consciously monumental character of many of the most important European remains has invited their destruction as a patriotic or an ideological duty in later ages. Down with the Bastille! Men who make icons prepare for the iconoclasts of the future: they are unwittingly preparing the most interestingly disfigured museum pieces. Protestant reformers dutifully defaced monuments of the Roman Catholic Church, fanatical rationalists in the time of the French Revolution smashed the heads off the statues of Notre Dame. Later emperors seek to erase the greater monuments of their predecessors—or, preferably, to carve their own names on them instead. Every ideologue tries to burn the ideologues who have gone before. In nations with oscillating histories it becomes a patriotic duty to destroy the embarrassingly inconsistent past. Signs of "Hitlerstrasse" or "Stalinallee" are covered by names advertising the current ideology. Revolutions and reformations leave only the few relics which are too solid to be moved or too holy to be touched.

But the American past is erased in a more casual and good-natured fashion. A house is removed to make way for a road; it is reconstructed to fit in the modern improvements: the two-car garage, the television room, or the air-conditioning. Except for the Indian destruction of early settlements, or the few wanton destructions by British troops during the American Revolution and the War of 1812 (which happened to include the White House), and such Civil War episodes as the burning of Atlanta and Sherman's march to the sea, the relics of the American past have been removed not to deny the past, but to fulfill and improve it. It is no wonder that Americans feel the need to manufacture historical monuments.

II.

These differences between our way of seeking our national past and of building our historical monuments and the European ways are vividly illustrated by a number of recent enterprises in historical reconstruction. Perhaps the most important of these is Colonial Williamsburg in Virginia, the project supported by about fifty million dollars of Mr. John D. Rockefeller, Jr.'s money, and by a great deal of his personal enthusiasm. This effort to restore and reconstruct an American colonial capital is only the largest of an increasing number of efforts (New Salem, Sleepy Hollow, Jamestown, and Old Sturbridge Village are others) to discover our past by rebuilding the communities and the scenes of everyday activity of an earlier age. These are a special kind of historical reconstruction and popular interpretation. They are not entirely without precedent in Europe (for example in the Norwegian Folk Museums), but in this country they have taken on an unprecedented importance and influence. Colonial Williamsburg is not only a brilliant example of an American style in historical monuments; it has become a school for training skilled professional interpreters who will be devotees of this American style.

Meanwhile, academic historians, disturbed by the heterodoxy, the boldness, and the popular appeal of Colonial Williamsburg, have generally not given it the significance it deserves. Some have been inclined to treat it as simply another example—like William Randolph Hearst's notorious imported castles—of a wealthy man indulging his whim. Some dismiss it as an educational "gadget" like the audio-visual aids to which they are unsympathetic. Or they treat it condescendingly as a harmless but amusing example of American vulgarity—a kind of patriotic Disneyland. But several visits there have persuaded me that it is significant in ways which its promoters did not advertise. Even before Colonial Williamsburg, the movies and radio had imposed specific tasks of historical verisimilitude on interpreters of our past which the historical novelist and stage-dramatist had been able to evade. Television has only increased these challenges and further widens the unprecedentedly vast popular audience for vivid presentations of daily life in the past. As a historical monument, Colonial Williamsburg and others of its school make a comparable effort at popular interpretation of our history. They are almost as American in their method as in their subject matter.

In the first place, Colonial Williamsburg is a strikingly democratic kind of national monument. It presumes an unspecialized and unaristocratic kind of education. Unless one already knows a great deal, one cannot learn much from visiting the Roman Forum or the Athenian Acropolis. The Capitoline Museum, the Prado, or the National Gallery in London, seem a jungle of canvas and marble to anyone not already instructed in the

different arts and periods represented. Each room
or department preserves the relics of only one kind
of art, and usually of that art in only a single
period. The European museum is a pretty esoteric
place. The untutored visitor whose main sensations
are of magnificence and discomfort considers himself lucky if he remembers the name of the museum.
The numerous palace-museums—like the Louvre,
Hampton Court, the Uffizi, the Pitti, or Schoen-
brunn—are not any more comfortable, although
they may be more interesting because they at least
show the common visitor where the rich and powerful used to live.

All such places are planned, and maintained
primarily for the connoisseur, the art collector, the
patron, the professor, or the scholar, not for the
citizen. Only in Pompeii (which was made by catastrophe and not on purpose, and which is usually
considered a curiosity rather than a major cultural
monument), can the unlearned, children, and lay-
men without a cultivated historical imagination
feel interested and at home.

But Colonial Williamsburg is a place where
people often go "because of the children." And because it offers not a segment of the history of a
particular fine art, but a model of a going community, it is intelligible and interesting to nearly
everybody. Nobody is a specialist in daily life! It is
a symbol of a culture where the fine arts have become much less important; where literacy is a
higher ideal than literariness. The forbidding rib-
bon across the antique chair, the "Do Not Touch"
sign, the somnolent guard (whose only qualifi-
cation is that he is a disabled war veteran)—these
omnipresent features of the European museum have

nothing to do with the American restored community. One of the most startling and impressive facts to anyone who has "done" Europe, is that the guides of Colonial Williamsburg have no set speeches, and are actually giving the visitor their own interpretation of the current lectures on colonial life, which the Director of Interpretation expects them to attend. Visitors have some sense of using what the colonials themselves used; they see how things worked.

A Colonial Williamsburg would be impossible in a country that was not wealthy. It is made for the prosperous millions; for the "middling sort" of Americans; for a nation of paved roads, and automobile owners and well-paid vacations, for a child-centered, newspaper-reading nation where families do things together. Colonial Williamsburg—like the American spelling bee, the strenuous effort to make college a "fun" experience, John Dewey's project method of education, educational television shows, and quiz shows—symbolizes the American refusal to segregate any kind of activity: the refusal to believe that education need be a chore, or that learning need be confined to solemn and studious hours. Business and pleasure *ought* to be combined. Colonial Williamsburg acquires its fully American character with the completion of its vast motel (with cafeteria and swimming pool) and information center (offering free films about the colonial period). Americans like to learn together, they like to enjoy their education. For all these purposes Colonial Williamsburg is perfectly suited and in a way which has no parallel.

How did so appropriate an expression of national

culture ever come into being? It was not the product of government initiative. Beginning partly as
an imaginative private whim, it could not have
been accomplished without shrewd real-estate deal-
ings, architectural ingenuity, applied archaeology,
and effective public relations. It is a spectacular
example of private enterprise at work in the creation of a national monument. Over thirty years
ago, Dr. W. A. R. Goodwin, a single-minded Episcopal minister who loved Williamsburg, conceived
the idea and fired the imagination of Mr. John D.
Rockefeller, Jr., who not only paid for it, but became foster father of the idea. It is not the product
of legislative or other committees, of log-rolling
or boondoggling, but of a few individuals who had
a queer and "impossible" idea. "Money was no
object." On one occasion when a particular house,
already partly reconstructed, had been built a few
feet from its precise original position, Mr. Rockefeller did not hesitate to spend six thousand dollars
to have it moved to its proper spot. Yet in the
midst of the restored village one finds a few islands
which have been left to their owners, because the
Committee has considered the prices asked for the
property to be exorbitant. The Virginia legislature
has co-operated, local historical societies have
helped. But Colonial Williamsburg vividly exemplifies the paradox that only in a wealthy country
can people care little about money.

Colonial Williamsburg is an American kind of
sacred document. It asserts the belief in the continuity of past and present. Such an attempt to
reconstruct the way of life of a whole past community and to interpret it to all living Americans
is not only more expensive, but vastly more difficult

and more taxing on the historical imagination, than to restore any particular ancient monument. The technical problems of archaeology have really turned out to be the least of all the problems.

III.

A number of questions which Colonial Williamsburg has posed to its restorers have expressed some large peculiarities of American history. The restorers of such a community must, in the first place, be willing to break out of respected academic conventions; they must be willing to risk the objections, and even the ridicule of pedants, and the misunderstanding of scholars, of self-styled sophisticates, and of cosmopolites who are accustomed to the very different monuments of Europe. They must not be afraid to be at the same time archaeological precisionists, dramatic producers, advertisers, and promoters; and even occasionally to look a little silly to the humorless academic eye. They must combine the techniques of Hollywood, Madison Avenue, Wall Street, and Schenectady with those of the universities, museums, and research libraries. This is an extraordinary concoction. But American culture is extraordinary; and anyone who would provide us our kind of national monument must not be afraid to mix things which elsewhere have not seemed to go together.

In the course of this effort, the builders and promoters of Colonial Williamsburg have faced special temptations. These are, in one sense, only the temptations of all searchers for the past. But they are made especially seductive by the peculiarities of American history, and by the special role of our history in our effort to discover ourselves.

The Temptation to Make the Past Too Homogeneous

At any one time every community is actually a hodgepodge of the relics of different periods. The architectural "unity" of any period exists only in the minds of architectural historians. No age completely consumes its buildings; only in the oldest or the newest settlements, or after a great conflagration like the Fire of London or the Chicago Fire, or in some of our contemporary projects of urban renewal or in suburban Levittowns and Park Forests are whole areas constructed in a single style. Thus the real look of a community in any particular period actually cannot be recaptured if its builders illustrate only one style. The reconstructor's temptation is to be too pure; and in his effort to catch the special flavor of one age he may forget the admixture of earlier ages which was vivid to the men who lived then. Even in Colonial Williamsburg this temptation has not been wholly resisted, if only in choosing "typical" buildings of the immediate prerevolutionary period for restoration. In the code of restoration principles adopted at the beginning of the work in 1928, the advisory committee wisely recommended that "All buildings or parts of buildings in which the colonial tradition persists should be retained irrespective of their actual date." Ironically, the modern and unrestored parts of the village, by adding a note of variety, actually help us recover some of the heterogeneity of the once-living community.

But the very peculiarities of our history which focus our interest on the "middling sort" of men, put difficulties in the way of a fully appropriate restoration. The grander buildings tend to be the more durable; they are the ones for which we have blueprints, insurance records, and the detailed comments of colonial travelers. Yet to find the flavor of Williamsburg as an American community we must recapture the ways of living of craftsmen, servants, small businessmen, and others whose houses left the least trace. The restorers of Williamsburg are, of course, aware of this difficulty; and in their reconstruction of several craft shops they have made an effort to overcome it. But they are inevitably the victims of the ephemeral character of the life they are trying to recapture; a way of life is always more complex, more mixed, and more elusive than any particular grand monument.

The Temptation to Make the Past Too Pretty

The restorer faces a dilemma: if he tries to camouflage his work by artificial weathering and machine-made wormholes, he becomes a kind of forger. But if he does not, he misleads the viewer by making the past seem too shipshape. The restorers of Williamsburg have followed the rule that "where new materials must be used, they should be of a character approximating the old as closely as possible, but no attempt should be made to 'antique' them by theatrical means." Walking through restored Williamsburg, one finds these authentic colonial buildings as neat and well painted as the houses in a new suburb; while only buildings of jarring modern design look weathered and lived in. In a few years restored buildings will have a more lived-in look (many of the houses are occu-

pied by the staff of Colonial Williamsburg and the
Institute of Early American History and Culture);
they will never have the shabbiness that many of
them must have shown in the colonial era. But this
fresh paint is a useful warning of the unbridgeable
gulf between past and present. It has the same advantage as the specially colored plaster used in
restoring European remains. The fresh paint and
newly applied wallpaper which discomfit the romantic visitor actually can help save Colonial Williamsburg from the tea room "quaintness" found
along New England highways. To the colonials
themselves, the buildings were, of course, anything
but quaint. They wished a look of orderly newness
(including a coat of expensive fresh paint) as much
as we do today.

The same kind of difficulty is presented by the
lack of odors which were among the most vivid
sensations of any colonial town. Yet if somehow
these odors could be recreated (as the restorers
might conceivably try in a building or two), they
would probably blot out everything else. We must
remember that body odors, and odors of food,
sewage, and cover-up perfume, were commonplace
to the age. Any large-scale effort to reproduce colonial smells would seem melodramatic, and would
actually destroy verisimilitude for twentieth-century
visitors. Odors were routine for Jefferson, Wythe,
and their contemporaries; revived today they would
seem more pungent and more offensive than they
ever did to them. This is only one of the many
ways in which even the most sensible and skillful
restorer is doomed (by his very success as a twentieth-century interpreter) to miss the precise
"aroma" of colonial life.

The Temptation to Make the Past Too Relevant

A good deal too much of the literature about Colonial Williamsburg tells us that the life of that day embodied the principles which we live by today. There is, of course, some truth in the explanation in the official guidebook of how "eighteenth-century Williamsburg embodied concepts of lasting importance to all men everywhere." The "five concepts" there listed include "the integrity of the individual," "responsible leadership," "self-government," "individual liberties," and "opportunity"; these were in one way or another actually expressed in the life of that Virginia town. But the Williamsburg experience ought to underline the dynamic and the federal character of American life, which is actually expressed in the differences between what each of these "concepts" meant to the citizens of Colonial Williamsburg and what they mean to us today, and even in the many little differences between their life and the life of their contemporaries in Boston or Philadelphia. To make Colonial Williamsburg the symbol of a bloodless, soilless abstraction—"World Freedom"—obscures many of the characteristic and permanently valuable features of Southern colonial institutions. If Colonial Williamsburg is to serve its historical as well as its patriotic purpose, it must dramatize the uniqueness of Southern and of colonial, as much as of all American, institutions. This can best be accomplished by allowing the accurately restored community to speak for itself and to speak concretely and in detail. This purpose was best expressed by Mr. Rockefeller himself when he explained: "I wasn't trying to recreate a lovely city,

nor was I interested in a collection of old houses.
I was trying to recreate Williamsburg as it stood
in the eighteenth century." This is a much more
honest and feasible educational purpose than to
make Colonial Williamsburg a didactic "example"
of political abstractions.

In their very efforts to deal with these problems,
the restorers of Colonial Williamsburg have told
us a great deal more about America, past and
present, than its founders ever imagined. If anyone
had set out thirty years ago to exemplify on a
grand scale the American approach to the national
past, he could hardly have done better.

5. THE DIRECT DEMOCRACY OF PUBLIC RELATIONS: SELLING THE PRESIDENT TO THE PEOPLE

In Europe the history-making political leaders have usually been set apart from the crowd by qualities of the artist and the prophet, but ours have generally been respectable spokesmen for the respectable community. Compare, for example, the place of Queen Elizabeth I, Cromwell, Robespierre, Napoleon, Bismarck, Hitler, Garibaldi, Mussolini, Lenin, or Stalin in their national traditions with that of William Bradford, John Winthrop, Benjamin Franklin, George Washington, Thomas Jefferson, Andrew Jackson, and Abraham Lincoln in ours. The most remembered and most adored European leaders have been erratic and charismatic, with at least a touch of the daemonic. Claiming the inspiration of God, they avow their desire to change the course of history. They are remembered as makers—not merely reflectors—of the spirit of their age. By contrast ours have been simply "representative men," possessing the commonplace virtues in extraordinary degree. Washington embodied the sober judgment and solid character of the Virginia planter. Andrew Jackson was only one of many elevated by the rise of the West. "This middle-class country," Emerson shrewdly remarked in his oration on Lincoln, "had got a middle-class president, at last."

As the power of the President and of the Federal Government increase, we should be troubled by whether the affairs of a great nation can be conducted by no better than a "typical" American. Perhaps we can no longer rely on that remarkable Providence (first observed by an enemy of Lincoln who foresaw Lincoln's election but had faith the nation would survive him) which has helped our nation outlive the most insipid leaders. We cannot look cheerfully on further temptations to apotheosize the commonplace in the most powerful office in the land.

Yet a number of facts, so recent and so peripheral to the familiar topics of political history that they have hardly begun to enter our textbooks, actually add up to just this. They offer new temptations for our national political leader to be a passive spokesman for the Voice of the People. They make it easier and more necessary than ever before that any candidate for the Presidency should seem constantly to have his hand on the public pulse. And they make it easier than ever for Americans to confuse vigorous leadership with adept followership.

These new tendencies could be described as the rise of the Nationally-Advertised President. Franklin Delano Roosevelt was our first. The attitude of the vast majority of the American people to him was as different from that of their grandfathers to the presidents of their day as our attitude to General Motors is different from that of our great-grandfathers to the village harness-maker. Like other "nationally-advertised brands," F.D.R. could not, of course, have been successful if he had not had something to offer. But he might not have been able to sell himself to the American public—on such a scale, and for twice as many terms as any of his predecessors—without the aid of certain revolutionary changes in our system of public communication.

I.

During the nineteenth century the telegraph transformed American journalism. Until the 1830's —that is, until the coming of the telegraph—the reporting of political news in the United States was a bitterly partisan business. Newspapers were owned body and soul by one or another political party, and, generally speaking, lacked moderation, conscience, or decency. The practice of ignoring or misrepresenting the opposition's statements was pushed to a point unknown today even among the most partisan of our large daily papers. Not until the last years of the age of Jackson did news begin to be sold in the open market, and as it became a commodity its quality began to improve. And with the rise of the cheap newspaper— the "penny press" in those days—addressed to a vast audience, newspapers tended to become financially independent of political parties. The growing volume of advertising they carried further encouraged them to assert their political independence.

It was the telegraph, of course, that made possible the establishment of enterprises—the wire services —selling news to newspapers (the AP was founded in 1848), and these had a financial interest in seeing a crudely partisan press supplanted by an independent one. The wire services sold a nonpartisan product; very early they set a standard of impartial reporting that still distinguishes our press from that of most of the rest of the world.

Technical and economic developments made it possible to communicate news to more and more people more rapidly than ever before. The Fourdrinier machine for producing paper in a continuous strip instead of in sheets, and the Hoe presses, which by around 1900 could produce up to 144,000 sixteen-page newspapers per hour, acted as both cause and effect in making the news big business. By the turn of the century, major newspaper chains like Scripps's and Hearst's were going strong. The great rise in newspaper circulation set in soon after 1892; in that year there were only ten papers in four cities that had a circulation of over one hundred thousand; by 1914 there were over thirty of that size in a dozen cities. During this period, the average circulation of daily newspapers in the United States just about doubled. The combined circulation of daily newspapers in 1930 amounted to over forty-four million; by 1955 the figure was nearly fifty-five million.

To this growing business the government, and especially the federal government in Washington, offered the richest single source of raw material. At the beginning of this century there were less than two hundred Washington correspondents. The number increased sharply during the First World War, but even in 1929 the Washington press bureaus were only about a third their present size. By 1952 about fifteen hundred people in

Washington made their living directly from collecting and reporting national news.

We sometimes forget that the Presidential press conference is an institution of very recent date. Only fifty years ago there were no regularly scheduled news conferences at the White House. From time to time, President Theodore Roosevelt, while being shaved, would allow Lincoln Steffens to ask him questions; and he was the one who first provided a special anteroom for White House correspondents. Under President Wilson, something like the present formal and regular White House press conferences first came into being. Although interrupted by the First World War, the institution was continued in one form or another by all presidents after him. The figure any one of these cut in newspapers all over the country depended very much on how he "handled himself" during these periodic interviews. F.D.R. was the first President to appoint a special press secretary, and the power of that office has steadily increased.

By the early twentieth century a continual, ever widening current of news was flowing from the White House. The news-gathering agencies themselves began to become self-appointed representatives of public opinion who put point-blank questions to the President, and from whom the President could learn what was troubling the public mind. Communication was now constant and two-way. No longer did the press await "statements" from the White House; it could prod the President when he was reticent, and focus attention on embarrassing questions. The corps of Washington correspondents became a more flexible, more regular, more direct, and at times more successful means than Congress itself of calling the President to public account.

The new continuity, informality, and immediacy of relations between people and President were furthered by the radio, which, with catastrophic suddenness, became a major factor in American political life during the twenties. The first Presidential election whose results were publicly broadcast was that of November 2, 1920: between five hundred and one thousand Americans were wearing earphones on that night to learn whether Harding or Cox had been elected. By 1922 about four hundred thousand radio sets were in use in the United States; by 1928 the number had increased more than twenty-fold to eight and a half million; in 1932 to eighteen million; by 1936 to thirty-three million; and by 1950 to well over eighty million. It was in the elections of 1924, however, that the radio began to acquire real political significance; in that year, for the first time, the proceedings of the two national party conventions were broadcast to the public. But not until 1928 did the major parties make extensive use of the radio in their campaigning, when for the first time millions of Americans heard the candidates' voices in their own homes. The inauguration of President Hoover, on March 4, 1929, was broadcast over a network of one hundred twenty stations.

These and other changes still to come in American political life were, of course, intimately connected with the rising American standard of living. For the ever accelerating need to cultivate the market to increase the wants of the people, and to attract them to specific products, was served by both press and radio. Advertising had begun to become big business by about the 1880's, but only in the last fifty years has its growth been spectacular. Until about 1890 most dailies still received more revenue from the sale of papers than from advertising; by 1914 advertising was providing many with two-thirds of their income, by 1929 with three-fourths. The bills that advertising clients received from radio stations amounted only to about five million dollars in 1927; the sum shot up to over one hundred and seven millions in 1936; by 1945 it was nearly four hundred and eighty millions; and in 1949 had increased by nearly another third, to the phenomenal figure of six hundred and thirty-seven millions. Advertising agencies in the United States, which handled a business of nearly six hundred million dollars in 1930, had an annual business in the neighborhood of a billion dollars about fifteen years later.

It is not surprising that the self-conscious and scientific study of public opinion, which was to become important in national political calculations by mid-century, had its roots in the efforts of advertisers to evaluate the reach of their advertising dollars. The first public opinion surveys were made by advertising managers to discover who was reading their copy. In 1919 there appeared the first survey department within an advertising agency, and the first independent surveying agency. It was not until 1935, however, that the representative sample method was used in public opinion surveys. In July of that year—in the middle of F.D.R.'s first administration—Elmo Roper published his first survey in *Fortune;* a few months later Dr. George Gallup began releasing his surveys as director of the American Institute of Public Opinion.

During this very period, a new philosophy and science of public opinion came into being. Walter Lippmann's *Public Opinion* (1922)—soon followed by his *Phantom Public* (1925)—advanced the important idea of "stereotypes" and explored some theoretical consequences of the new publicity. For the citizen was now becoming more and more like the customer. With the characteristic American directness, a new profession of "public relations" developed. The anti-big business sentiment of the 1880's and 1890's and the rise of muckraking had disposed big business men to offer high prices for skillful press-agentry. Ivy Lee, by paying some attention to the public interest and to the legitimate curiosity of newspaper reporters, helped put this new activity on a respectable (and profitable) footing. "This profession," observed Edward L. Bernays in the foreword to his *Crystallizing Public Opinion* (1923), "in a few years has developed from the status of circus agent stunts to . . . an important position in the conduct of the world's affairs."

By the time that Franklin Delano Roosevelt came into office on March 4, 1933, technological and institutional innovations had in many ways prepared the way for a transformation of the relation between President and people. Communications from the President to the reading or listening public, which formerly had been ceremonial, infrequent, and addressed to small audiences, could now be constant, spontaneous, and directed to all who could read or hear (sometimes whether they wished to or not). And now through the questions put to the President at his regular press conferences, and through the telegrams and mail received after his radio addresses or public statements, he could sense the temper and gauge the drift of public opinion— he could find out what the sovereign people wanted. He could even send up trial balloons to get some advance idea of public response to his future decisions. The President was no longer simply dealing with the "people," but with "public opinion."

There is no denying that F.D.R. possessed a genius for using these means of communication. Without them he could hardly have developed that novel intimacy between people and President which marked his administrations. In the little memorial miscellany published by Pocket Books on April 18, 1945 (less than a week after F.D.R.'s death), we read in Carl Carmer's verse dialogue:

> Woman:
> . . . Come home with me
> If you would think of him. I never saw him—
> But I knew him. Can you have forgotten
> How, with his voice, he came into our house,
> The President of these United States,
> Calling us friends. . . .
> Do you remember how he came to us
> That day twelve years ago—a little more—
> And you were sitting by the radio
> (We had it on the kitchen table then)
> Your head down on your arms as if asleep.

For the first time in American history the voice of the President was a voice from kitchen tables, from the counters of bars and lunchrooms, and the corners of living rooms.

F.D.R.'s relaxed and informal style, both in writing and speaking, enabled him to make the most
of the new informal circumstances under which
people heard him. That he was compelled by his
infirmity to sit while giving his radio talks only
added to the informality. A whole world separates
F.D.R.'s speeches from those of his immediate
predecessors—from the stilted rhetoric of the oratory collected in such volumes as Calvin Coolidge's
Foundations of the Republic (1926) or Herbert
Hoover's *Addresses Upon the American Road*
(1938). Earlier Presidential speeches had too often
echoed the style and sentiments of commencement
addresses; F.D.R. could say something informal and
concrete even in such an unpromising State Paper
as a "Mother's Day Proclamation."

Perhaps never before had there been so happy a
coincidence of personal talent with technological
opportunity as under his administrations. In the
eight volumes of the *Public Papers and Addresses
of Franklin D. Roosevelt,* which cover the era of
the New Deal, we discover two new genres of political literature which were the means by which a
new relationship between President and people was
fashioned. The first genre was established in tran-
scriptions of Presidential press conferences; the
second, in F.D.R.'s radio talks, the "fireside chats."
Both are distinguished by an engaging casualness
and directness; but this is not all that makes them
new genres in the literature of American politics.
Here, for the first time among Presidential papers,
we find an extensive body of public utterances that
are unceremonial yet serious.

Only a year after F.D.R. assumed office, Theodore
G. Joslin, who had handled press relations for

President Hoover, observed that President Roosevelt had already come nearer than any of his predecessors "to meeting the expectations of the four hundred men and women who, in these times of stress, write half a million words a day to bring to our firesides news of developments at the seat of the Government." F.D.R. had already shown the camaraderie and the willingness to make news which made some correspondents (not always his political friends) call his administration a "new deal for the press." The unprecedented frequency of his press conferences established a continuity of relations with both correspondents and the reading public. During Hoover's administration there had been only sixty-six Presidential press conferences; but F.D.R held three hundred thirty-seven press conferences during his first administration, and three hundred seventy-four during his second. Thus, while Hoover met the press on an average of less than once in every three weeks, Roosevelt would see them about five times in that same period. The record of his conferences shows how this frequency bred intimacy, informality, and a set of institutionalized procedures; before long the spirit of those press conferences became on both sides much like that of any other responsible deliberative body.

Similarly, the frequency with which the President went on the air effected a revolutionary change. Between March and October 1933, F.D.R. gave four "fireside chats." Through these, for the first time in American history, a President was able to appeal on short notice and in his own voice to the whole constituency. Neither the press conference nor the "fireside chat" was an occasion for *ex cathedra* pronouncements. On the contrary, they were designed to stimulate a more active "dialogue" between the people and the Chief Executive.

Perhaps the best index of the effect of F.D.R.'s radio talks was the volume of White House mail. In McKinley's time Presidential mail amounted to about a hundred letters a day, which were handled by a single clerk. Despite occasional flurries at inaugurations or crises, the daily flow remained small. Not until President Hoover's time did its volume increase significantly. Even then letters sometimes did not number more than a few hundred a day, and the system of handling them remained unchanged. Under F.D.R., however, Presidential mail acquired a new and unprecedented volume, as we learn from the reminiscences of Ira R. T. Smith, for many years chief Presidential mail clerk (*"Dear Mr. President . . .": The Story of Fifty Years in the White House Mail Room*):

Mr. Roosevelt always showed a keen interest in the mail and kept close watch on its trend. Nothing pleased him more than to know that I had to build up a big staff and often had to work until midnight to keep up with a run of 5000 to 8000 letters a day, and on some occasions many more thousands. He received regular reports. . . . Whenever there was a decrease in the influx of letters we could expect to hear from him or one of his secretaries, who wanted to know what was the matter—was the President losing his grip on the public?

Before F.D.R. came to the White House, Mr. Smith had handled all the mail by himself. But when, in response to his First Inaugural Address, F.D.R. received over four hundred fifty thousand letters, it was plain that a new era had begun. During certain periods as many as fifty persons were required to open and sort the White House mail; before long an electric letter-opener was installed, and instead of the old practice of counting individual pieces of mail, Mr. Smith and his helpers began measuring stacked-up letters by the yard.

Also, a new self-consciousness governed F.D.R.'s communications to the public; the era of "public relations" had begun. It was not enough that the President (or someone else for him) should state what he really believed—one had to consider all the "angles." Andrew Jackson had had his Amos Kendall and his Frank Blair; and it had not been uncommon for Presidents to employ ghost writers and close personal advisers who, in some cases, were responsible for both style and content. But perhaps never before did a President depend so consistently and to such an extent in his literary product on the collaboration of advisers. Among F.D.R.'s speech-writers were men like Harry Hopkins, Robert Sherwood, Samuel Rosenman, Stanley High, Charles Michelson, Ernest Lindley, Sumner Welles, Raymond Moley, Rexford Tugwell, Archibald MacLeish, Tom Corcoran, Basil O'Connor, and Robert Jackson—and these are only a few. F.D.R.'s speeches, even the most important and those seemingly most personal, were as much a co-operative product as a piece of copy produced by a large advertising agency. The President's genius consisted very much in his ability to give calculated, prefabricated phrases an air of casualness. It was, of course, remarkable that his speeches retained any personal flavor at all. And it was significant that this collaborative literary activity was not kept secret. The public began to take it as much for granted that the utterances of a President should be a composite product as that an advertisement of the Ford Motor Company should not be written by Henry Ford.

II.

In the longer perspective of American history, these changes that F.D.R., aided by technology, brought about in the conduct of the Presidency may become permanent and take on the quality of mutations.

The Decline in the Periodicity of American Political Life

In the early years of the Republic, politics—or at least national politics—was a "sometime thing." Political interest would rise to fever pitch before national elections or in times of crisis, and tend to subside in between. The very vastness of the country reinforced this tendency to periodicity in American political life. And so our elections became notorious for their barbecue, holiday atmosphere: brief but hectic interruptions of the routine of life.

But the technological developments which I have described increased the President's opportunity, and eventually his duty, to make news. Now headlines could be produced at an hour's notice. To oblige the correspondents by making big stories frequently, and small stories constantly, became part of his job. In F.D.R.'s era, of course, the crises in economic life and international affairs were themselves rich raw material for the press. There had been crises and wars before, but never before had so large and steady a stream of announcements, information, "statements to the press," and description of "problems facing the country" poured from the headquarters of government. The innocent citizen now found no respite from this barrage of politics and government. Even over a beer at his favorite bar he was likely to hear the hourly news broadcast, or the very voice of his President.

The citizen was no longer expected to focus his attention only temporarily on a cluster of issues (conveniently dramatized by two rival personalities) at the time of national election. With the rise of the weekly news magazine (*Time* was founded in 1923, *Newsweek* in 1933), of news quizzes, news broadcasts, and radio forums, the citizen was given a new duty, that of being "well informed." The complex of alphabetical agencies, the intricate and remote problems of foreign policy, and the details of the legislative process came now, as never before, to burden his mind and plague his conscience. Whether or not the American citizen was consciously becoming more "political," he was surely finding it more and more difficult to escape politics. No longer was he granted the surcease of inter-election periods when his representatives were left to their own devices and he could turn to other things. Paradoxically, in spite of the great increase in population, the national government was becoming less and less republican, and more and more democratic; for elected officials were now in more constant touch with their constituencies.

Increased Communication between the People and the President

The very agencies that the President was now using to communicate his views to the public were also employed to elicit the public's response. Letters to the President—and to Congressmen—became a special American version of the ancient right of

petition. As communications to public officials mul-
tiplied, the temptations increased for the public
official, and especially the President, to trim his sails
to the shifting winds of opinion, which now sometimes blew with hurricane force into Washington
offices. The weak representative or the demagogue
would find it easier to be weak and yet to seem to
be strong by following the majority view at every
turn. Here was still another force to prevent the
realization of Burke's ideal of the independent representative, and to make him a "mere" spokesman
of popular views.

The Decline of Naïveté

The efflorescence of "public relations" techniques
and of opinion polls increased the temptation for
the President to rely on experts in dealing with the
public. Even if Presidential utterances would still
have the appearance of casualness, it would be a
studied casualness, or one that the people would
suspect of being studied. The President would scru-
tinize surveys of press opinions; he would employ
(sometimes within the very agencies of government)
specialists in "opinion research" to inform him of
what the people liked or disliked. He would employ
theatrical advisers to help him find his most appealing voice and posture before the television
cameras. In these ways, the citizen was more and
more assimilated to the customer; he had to be
"approached," his responses had to be measured
so that he could be given what he wanted, or
thought he wanted.

The Inversion of Geographic and Political Distances

The new developments in communications made many of the oldest assumptions about the relations between geography and politics irrelevant. Jefferson and his "States Rights" disciples had started from the axiom that the citizen's knowledge and hence his capacity for an informed opinion were in inverse ratio to his geographic distance from the headquarters of decision. The closer he was to the scene, the more he would presumably know, and the more exact would be his knowledge. Thus the average citizen was expected to be best informed about the political affairs of his municipality, only a little less informed about those of his state, and considerably less informed about the affairs of the nation as a whole. The changes that reached their climax under F.D.R. not only exploded this assumption, they came close to making it the reverse of the truth. Both the multiplication of newscasts and the expansion of the profession of radio and television news-commentator have focused attention on national events—since these are sure to interest the largest number of listeners; and audience volume decides where money will be invested in communications. National affairs have become more and more a good thing for the commercial sponsors of newscasts. Inevitably, many of the ablest reporters, too, have been attracted to the national capital. The citizen, when he listens to the news from Washington, now has the benefit of sophisticated, well-informed, and competent interpreters who seldom have equals in the state capitals or on the local scene.

There thus has developed a new disparity between the quality and quantity of information about national as contrasted with state or local matters. By about 1940, largely owing to the press and the radio, the citizenry had already reached a point where it was better informed about national than about local issues. This reversal of a long-standing assumption, which was not just a result of the marked increase in federal activities under the New Deal, will require revision of accepted notions about federalism, and about the competence of the average citizen to participate in government.

We are already far enough from the age of F.D.R. to begin to see that the tendencies which I have just described were not ephemeral. American experience under F.D.R. created new expectations that continue to clamor for fulfillment. When we look on into the administrations of Truman and Eisenhower, we see that these expectations became institutionalized. F.D.R. had set a style that later Presidential candidates could only at their peril violate. President Truman's success and the defeat of Governor Dewey in the 1948 elections cannot be explained unless such novel factors are taken into account. The growth of television, and its frequent (and on the whole successful) use by President Eisenhower, only carry further the tendencies initiated in the age of F.D.R. While later Presidents might lack the vividness of F.D.R.'s personality, perhaps never again would any man attain the Presidency or discharge its duties satisfactorily without entering into an intimate and conscious relation with the whole public. This opens unprecedented opportunities for effective and en-

lightening leadership. But it also opens unprecedented temptations. For never before has it been
so easy for a statesman to seem to lead millions
while in reality tamely echoing their every shifting
mood and inclination.

6. SOME AMERICAN DISCONTENTS

Unlike most modern nations, which only gradually acquired their sense of identity, we Americans started in the early nineteenth century with an aggressive assertion of our absolute distinctness from all the world. We bragged of being Americans without being able to say just what we meant; anyone who reads Emerson and Whitman cannot fail to sense both the insistence and the vagueness. The two formal elements in that sense of identity were: a belief in our "differentness" from all the world; and a belief in our physical separateness from all the world. Together they comprise the belief in American uniqueness.

Since about 1900 we have begun to discover that in many unsuspected ways we might be like the world and might be involved with the world. This declining sense of American uniqueness is the great trauma of the American mind in the last half-century. It has stirred our dissatisfaction with ourselves by shattering our traditional self-image. It has deprived us of our orientation toward the world. It has made us wonder who we really are. It is as if the Athenians had suddenly begun to doubt whether they were unlike the Spartans, or the

Romans to suspect that they were really barbarians at heart.

All this has made us discontented, both with ourselves for not remaining happily the way we had always been, and with the world for assimilating us. It has also made us feel guilty. Democratic institutions everywhere provide people with novel opportunities for self-reproach by shifting the responsibility for misfortunes from the people's rulers to themselves. We Americans told ourselves for many generations that we inhabited an earthly paradise. If things don't go well in paradise—in "God's Country"—the inhabitants themselves certainly must be at fault.

The facts which contradicted both our differentness and our insulation from the world seem in retrospect to be the main events of recent American history. The disappearance of the frontier, which Frederick Jackson Turner noted in 1893, only gradually received general recognition. The decline of immigration from Europe and the stability of the American population as a whole were legislated into reality by 1921. The Great Depression of 1929 fractured our myth of immunity to serious economic diseases. Meanwhile, of course, our involvement in the First World War, when we for the first time sent a large expeditionary force overseas and became thoroughly entangled in European diplomacy, had destroyed our political insularity. The European War Debts once and for all enmeshed us in the business of Europe: who can believe that he lives in a different world from that of his debtor? The New Deal borrowed heavily from European concepts of government. The lesson of the Second World War could have been more emphatic only if the continental United States had actually been attacked. Now nuclear weapons threaten to blast the remnant of our uniqueness.

These facts were the Fall of the American Adam. The American gradually discovered that he was no longer living in the Garden of Eden. How had it all happened? What was he to do about it? Should he try to recapture his Innocence, or should he try to atone for his Fall? These are the deep questions which have come to disturb the American mind and conscience.

American man had been, in John Henry's phrase, "the natchal man." He had been in many ways doctrinally naked; but he had not noticed it. Nor was he apologetic or ashamed until he tasted the sins and weaknesses of all mankind. Then—that is to say in the early twentieth century—he began frantically to seek a doctrine to cover his nakedness. It was thus the loss of our feeling of the "givenness" of our values that led us to a serious and general search for an "American Philosophy."

Europeans have naturally been inclined to classify American opinion into "isolationist" or "interventionist." But the basic categories stem not from our attitude toward Europe but from our attitudes toward ourselves and toward the puzzle of our own identity. Generally speaking, there have been three kinds of articulate individuals.

First, there are the "Singulists," those who deny the fact of our lost uniqueness. For them, the United States remains singular among all the nations of the world. Their irritability, their bad temper, and their belligerency all betray an inward suspicion that perhaps there is some substance to the sneaking doubt that America isn't as singular as she used to be. What they say is neither novel nor subtle; to the unsuspecting ear it recalls Washington's Farewell Address, Jefferson's First Inaugural, and the Monroe Doctrine. But by their rhetoric, the vagueness of their arguments, and their heavy reliance on slogan and sentiment, the Singulists betray their belief that American uniqueness can be perpetuated by the mere act of affirming it. They have adopted the Emil Coué fad of the 1920's and tell themselves: "Every day in every way we are getting to be more and more the way we've always been."

Who are these Singulists? They are all the groups and individuals who believe in the surviving innocence of the original American character. Among organizations they are the American Legion, the Daughters of the American Revolution, and a host of patriotic groups with large memberships. Among individuals they include the late publisher of the *Chicago Tribune,* Col. Robert R. McCormick, and such columnists as George Sokolsky and Westbrook Pegler. While superficially they might seem complacent, actually they are profoundly discontented with America, and with the drift of recent history. Like those who thought that Soviet Russia and Communist China could be wished out of existence by simply refusing to "recognize" them, the Singulists try to wish away the most disturbing facts of twentieth century American history by refusing to "recognize" them.

Perhaps the surest earmark of this point of view is an insistence on "100 per cent Americanism." It is the familiar overcompensation whose symptom is the superlative. The response of Hitlerite Germany to the weakness of their postwar position was that they were the strongest nation in the world. So the response of the Singulists to the suspicion that the United States may have lost some of her old uniqueness is to insist that we are "more unique" than ever before. From this point of view (contrary to European notions) recent "isolationism" is not essentially an expression of provincialism, materialism, or meanness of spirit. It is rather the frenetic response of people who have become accustomed to attribute everything good in their life to the uniqueness of their situation, and who feel that uniqueness in peril. This spirit, first expressed in the 1920's and 1930's in the form of articulate and self-conscious "isolationism," now is expressed also in anti-Communism; which is currently the most obvious way of insisting on American distinctness from a world seen as either controlled or about to be controlled by Communism.

The Singulists reaffirm American uniqueness by insisting that we are no less separate geographically and militarily than we ever were. We must make the Western Hemisphere a fortress against all the world, they argue. In diplomacy, it means that we can still "go it alone." They believe that we can keep separate from the world by certain acts of American policy, e.g., by keeping our money and our soldiers at home. Such devices as the constitutional amendment that Senator Bricker proposed in 1952 would supposedly perpetuate our insulation (and hence our virtue) by preventing the President from entangling us in the undergrowth of world diplomacy. The most intelligent and most honorable statements of the Singulist position in American foreign policy have been those of Senator William E. Borah in the 1920's and of the late Senator Robert Taft in the 1930's and 40's. Generally speaking, the Singulists have been against participation in the United Nations, and have opposed foreign aid programs.

They also continue to insist on the essential difference between our "Way of Life" in government and economics and the ways of life of all people elsewhere. Thus, Singulists like the late Senator Taft and Senator Dirksen have denied that the changing circumstances of American life and of world history in the last two generations have changed very much the appropriateness of old ways of dealing with domestic problems. They overlook the connection between the peculiar circumstances of the nineteenth century and our freedom from labor organization and from governmental interference. To them the totality of American uniqueness in that age seems a unit of inseparable elements all of which can and ought to be perpetuated.

The Singulists have been harassed by paradoxes. They love a vigorous young America, but they are tempted to keep her so by paralysis. Since empiricism, dynamism, pluralism, and restlessness have accounted for many of the institutions that have made America great, the most un-American thing we can do is to try to keep America exactly as it has always been. The Singulists fail to see this.

Take, for example, their attitude to immigration. For nearly a century after the founding of the nation the Federal government had not exercised its powers to restrict immigration. In 1882, Congress began to restrict Oriental immigration; in 1917 it initiated a series of acts restricting all immigration. These acts aimed to maintain the "purity" of the American population; but in one way after another they violated the spirit of the American tradition. The literacy test for immigrants finally adopted over President Wilson's veto in 1917 and the growing number of other tests—culminating in the McCarran Act of 1952—have tried to ensure that all immigrants are antiseptic, lacking in dangerous diseases and dangerous ideas. These are the furthest possible departure from our traditional policy, which Emma Lazarus inscribed under the Statue of Liberty. By 1940 the Singulists for whom Congressman Martin Dies spoke in his *Trojan Horse in America,* could see only such facts as that 90 per cent of the members of the American Communist Party were foreign-born. They repeated with alarm what had been the boast of Americans for decades, that "this is the only country in the world that will admit aliens to any considerable degree."

Or take civil liberties. The view of the Singulists (with certain honorable exceptions) is that the pristine America can be preserved only by prohibiting heterodoxy. Their novel view of our ancient liberties is expressed in the aphorism of a former governor of California who declared: "Freedom of speech is such a precious privilege, we must be careful to whom we give it." They have demanded loyalty oaths and have sought a dogma of Americanism for a country whose dogma has been anti-dogmatism.

Secondly there are the Universalists. Like the Singulists, the Universalists tend toward an extreme. They are discontented with us because we have not yet become one with mankind. Their point of view is well expressed in the shrill title of Stringfellow Barr's pamphlet, "Let's Join the Human Race" (1950). They respond to our loss of uniqueness with enthusiasm.

Generally, the Universalists are more "respectable" intellectually. The Singulists lean toward provincialism and at their worst are Know-Nothings, friendly toward xenophobia and chauvinism. The Universalists are cosmopolitans, at their worst leaning toward vague humanitarianism, megalomania, and romantic optimism. If the Singulists sometimes are anti-intellectual, the Universalists often are hyper-intellectual. The Singulists validate their position by "horse-sense" and the common experience of all Americans; the Universalists support their arguments by metaphysics, by Plato and Aristotle, by Great Books in foreign languages and from distant places. While the Singulists criticize us for not talking exclusively to ourselves, the Universalists criticize us for not talking to everybody else all the time. For the Singulist most problems of public policy could be settled by a conversation (preferably in the Middle West) between two ordinary Americans over a Coca-Cola: for the Universalist our problems would be better settled in a salon.

While the eyes of the Singulists are fixed on The Good Old Days, those of the Universalists look towards the Millennium. Neither focuses on history. One suffers from myopia, the other from far-sightedness; a clear view of the middle distance is not for them.

The Universalist position is most clearly expressed in foreign policy. At the extreme they demand immediate World Government. They have published a journal, *Common Cause,* and have actually issued a draft constitution for planetary federalism. The more moderate Universalists approved Clarence Streit's *Union Now,* and are now uncritically enthusiastic for the United Nations. Organizations like the Foreign Policy Association support them. Their intellectual lineage goes back to Wilson's aspiration "to make the world safe for democracy," to the movements of the 1920's and 1930's toward Peace and Disarmament.

Only a few extremists demand world government tomorrow, but more than a few Americans now accept the belief in "One World," which Wendell L. Willkie, Republican candidate for President in the election of 1940, expressed in his widely read book of that title. "There are no distant points in the world any longer . . . ," he wrote in 1943. "The myriad millions of human beings of the Far East are as close to us as Los Angeles is to New York by the fastest trains. I cannot escape the conviction that in the future what concerns them must concern us, almost as much as the problems of the people of California concern the people of New York."

From the Universalists we hear panicky and hysterical attacks on nationalism. "We must aim," they say, "at a federal constitution of the world, a working world-wide legal order, if we hope to prevent an atomic World War." Between the simple alternatives of World Government and World Catastrophe, there is no room for inconvenient realities like history. Nationalism becomes a dirty word. This point of view, elaborated in Emery Reves' *Anatomy of Peace* (1945), was endorsed in a letter signed by a remarkably varied group of Americans including Senators Fulbright, Pepper, and Elbert D. Thomas, ex-Justice Owen D. Roberts, an Episcopal Bishop, a prominent Jesuit, the publisher Mr. Gardner Cowles, Albert Einstein, Dorothy Canfield Fisher, Christopher Morley, Carl Van Doren, Mark Van Doren, a well-known labor leader, and others. "The modern Bastille is the nation-state," cries Mr. Reves, "no matter whether the jailers are conservative, liberal or socialist. The symbol of our enslavement must be destroyed if we ever want to be free again. The great revolution for the liberation of man has to be fought all over again." This position is especially attractive because it is so "revolutionary" that it requires no immediate action.

Generally speaking, the Universalists take for granted that our entrance into the world community implies our domestic assimilation to the politics of Europe. To trace the growth of these tendencies we would have to go back at least as far as President Wilson, whose "New Freedom" required means of governmental regulation more familiar in Europe than in America, and whose own conception of the Presidency was very close to that of a European prime minister. Under the New Deal these tendencies were accelerated. If, like Europe, we could suffer from disastrous depression, then maybe we should try some of the European expedients. Now for the first time in American history the intellectual and the academic had a position in government comparable to that of their fellow intellectuals in Europe. Wasn't this a good thing? It was hard for professors sitting comfortably near the throne to doubt that it was. Communism was, of course, an extreme form of Universalism; and the Communists had some success in persuading people to forget the uniqueness of American life in favor of the world panaceas of Marx and Lenin.

The Universalists began to discover that most of the traditional American virtues were in fact vices: our empiricism was an ignorance of philosophy, our vocationalism was philistinism, our wealth was materialism, and our widespread literacy was nothing but vulgarity. As early as the 1920's Irving Babbitt and his New Humanists attacked our material well-being as itself a vice, apologized for Henry Ford and Thomas A. Edison, and endorsed *Punch's* aphorism that the United States was not a country but a picnic. Later, in the 1930's and 1940's, Mortimer Adler and Robert Maynard Hutchins denied the fact of universal American literacy; they demanded that the subject matter of American education be redefined. They came more and more to think of educating Americans as training them to converse with the cultivated men of Europe and about European classics. Their target, of course, was John Dewey, who had sought to relate education to experience, and thereby to make the variety and the challenge of America even more important than books. The followers of this school sought structure, dogma, and unity. In order to think, Americans would have to learn to speak the universal language of the World's One-Hundred-and-Two Great Ideas. American thought, to be wise, would have to cease to be characteristically American.

Instead of being pleased with American welfare as the reward of skill, virtue, or good luck, they wrote of it shamefacedly as if it were a mark of sin, dishonesty, or prodigality. Did it not separate us from the fraternity of men? "The United States," Stringfellow Barr observed, "is a rich suburb, surrounded by slums." Shame on us for enjoying wealth in the midst of such poverty! For being so healthy while others are so diseased! For being so well-fed while others go hungry! Some of them called for a "World Development Authority" to spread the wealth of the world in a satisfactorily uniform layer. A well-meaning American, inspired by charity or by moderate schemes for improving the lot of men in particular places, was made to feel like a society matron in a mink coat taking a Christmas turkey to the deserving poor.

In both Singulists and Universalists we find depressive pessimism and manic optimism. The Singulists cry woe to the U.S.A. We will lose our democratic way of life, our prosperity, and all our virtues if we do not return at once to our original purity! The Universalists cry woe to the world. It is, they say, "ten minutes to midnight"! If today we don't make ourselves one with the world, catastrophe will be on us tomorrow. Both groups are romantically optimistic, although on different scales: one imagines return to a virginal old New World; the other imagines the approach of a millennial, perpetually peaceful, new Old World.

The most notable common quality, not only of these extremists but of all who are deeply shaken by the loss of American uniqueness, is a flight into dogma. The Singulists, from the nature of their position and of their following, have found less need to elaborate their intellectual foundations.

They are satisfied by patriotic slogans, for they suspect that "philosophy" itself is a European import. Even the philosophers of conservatism in America get pretty rough treatment at their hands. On the whole, therefore, the quest for doctrine is more notable among Universalists than among Singulists. Some have found it in religion, in a facile criticism of prevailing American religious attitudes. Others have found it in economics. The conservative philosophers must be included among the Universalists. Such sophisticated defenders of free enterprise as Henry Simon, Professor Milton Friedman, and Professor Friedrich Hayek, whose *Road to Serfdom* has been widely read, argue from a basically Universalist position. America, they say, needs free enterprise, not because it is the indigenous "American Way," but because recent European history shows that it ought to be the way for men everywhere. Russell Kirk's conservatism, as embodied in his book, *The Conservative Mind*, while less realistic, is also Universalist in urging that the evils of American life are to be remedied, not by returning to the way *we* ever were, but rather by reaching for what an aristocratic Europe used to be. Another group, represented by Arthur Schlesinger, Jr., and W. W. Crosskey, has reached back into the American past—to the Age of Jackson or the Framing of the Constitution—to validate what proves to be a New Deal Philosophy. The "New Conservatism" of Peter Viereck starts with the common problems of men everywhere, with how much we can learn from Metternich, and with a warning that in the United States we have not recognized our kinship with all men. From all sides we are exhorted to leap into explicitness.

The American Singulists and Universalists are, if anything, too well known in Europe (and especially in England). Too few Europeans are aware of the importance of a third and growing point of view in the United States. The exponents of this point of view I call "Pluralists." They are aware that we are and have always been only one among many nations; and they respect differences. Their attitude is neither chauvinistic nor optimistic but surgical. They view the loss of American uniqueness as a neutral fact, calling for neither indignation nor enthusiasm. And this is precisely why many Americans have found their point of view irritating. Nobody likes to be told to "keep calm." Moreover, when the Pluralists tell us that, they deny us our heroic role and even the more moderate satisfaction of living in some great "Age of Transition."

The view of the Pluralists is basically historical. They see history as a continuum. They do not expect that men or nations are ever likely to change much; and certainly not suddenly. They are not alarmed by recent history, for they are not obsessed by the uniqueness of the American past, and they remind us that we have never been quite as unique as we have supposed.

They urge self-analysis. It is not surprising, they explain, that we should feel sensitive and even a little guilty about our innocence. Unlike the countries of Europe, we have never been conquered or occupied by a foreign enemy, nor as a nation suffered the humiliation of "reconstruction." If we realize that we have been a poor little rich boy without the advantage of a rough-and-tumble youth, will this not itself help us understand ourselves and what others think of us? The Pluralists remind us that if we are to understand the common ways of mankind we must make up in imagination what we have missed in experience.

They show us how we have mistaken the fortunate characteristics of life on our own continent for universal characteristics of life on this planet. Reinhold Niebuhr, in his *Irony of American History* (1952), explains to us how the facts of our past have led us to believe in our own innocence as well as the innocence of the world. Professor C. Vann Woodward in his brilliant "Irony of Southern History" gives still subtler relevance to Niebuhr's insight. He urges us to exploit the variant histories of different sections of our country: for example, the Southern States during and after the Civil War shared common European experiences. These Pluralists see our hope, not in denying the past nor in affirming the future, but in understanding ourselves, accepting both the unique and the universal in our character. "America," Professor Woodward observes, "has had cynical disparagement of her ideals from foreign, unfriendly, or hostile critics. But she desperately needs criticism from historians of her own who can penetrate the legend without destroying the ideal, who can dispel the illusion of pretended virtue without denying the genuine virtues."

This has required a reinterpretation of our diplomatic past. Walter Lippmann attempted this in his *U.S. Foreign Policy: Shield of the Republic* (1943) and has been developing a Pluralist interpretation ever since. Perhaps most important are the writings of George F. Kennan, and especially his monumental study of Soviet-American relations during the Russian Revolution. He shows how our special circumstances have induced us to take certain attitudes toward ourselves and our foreign policy; and finally insists on the irrelevance and perils of many of those ideals and techniques in our new situation. Our traditionally "legalistic-moralistic" approach to international problems, he warns, is dangerous and fraught with illusions—illusions nourished by our peculiar history. "The idea of the subordination of a large number of states to an international juridical régime, limiting their possibilities for aggression and injury to other states, implies that these are all states like our own, reasonably content with their international borders and status." He reminds us how much we have lived by these illusions and shows how tolerant of us providence has been.

The Pluralists oppose the simplistic interpretations which we inherit from the days of the Nye Committee, and from Walter Millis' accounts of war as the product of warmongering. The revisionist view of the causes of the First World War, developed in the late 1920's by Sidney B. Fay, has prepared us to wonder whether we have really been as innocent as we suspected. "Power politics," they explain, is not a European superstition but is one of the basic facts of life. Perhaps the most influential and effective spokesman of this point of view has been Professor Hans Morgenthau, who urges on us the ideal of "peace through accommodation." His *Politics Among Nations* has had wide influence. The growing influence of this Pluralist point of view is suggested by the fact that Alf M. Landon, Republican candidate for President in 1936, could address the Kiwanis Club of Topeka, Kansas, only a few years ago urging them to keep an "open mind" on the possible admission of Red China to the United Nations.

In domestic politics the Pluralists are both less uniform and less dogmatic than either the Singulists or the Universalists. They start neither with a rigid demand to preserve a particular set of economic arrangements, nor with any predilection for the methods of European domestic politics. They are not alarmed by new expedients, nor do they automatically prefer them. They simply warn us against being obsessed either by our uniqueness or by the perils to it. The great enemy of nations, they say, is illusion. Satisfied by moderate objectives, they unashamedly plead for defense of the national interest.

In the United States today there is no widespread discontent with democracy; we still believe its promises. But we are discontented with ourselves and worried over our ability to fulfill those promises. Especially because we know that America has offered a peculiar opportunity for fulfillment. In other ways, too, we pay the price for having bragged so loudly of our identity before we had filled it with a specific content. We are tempted into negative and shifting definitions: to assume that we are simply what Europe is not. When Europe was aristocratic, we were simply anti-aristocratic; now that part of Europe is Communist, we are simply anti-Communist. But what are we, in and for ourselves?

If America had been smaller or less varied our problem might now be simpler and the remedies for our discontent easier. But when our identity was unquestioned and our uniqueness seemed absolute, all the forces of climate, geography, and economics confirmed our illusions. America was a world. We therefore came to misconceive, not only our own nature, but even the nature of the real world outside. When we finally emerged into the world, we expected the world to be like the womb. Some of our deepest and most unnecessary disappointments have come from this naïve expectation.

If it is hard for us to live with the fact that the world is not simply a larger America, we should find some solace in the providential irony that defeats every idea once it becomes universal. If the world should ever become democratic perhaps none of it could remain so. Who would then be the critics of democracy? For whom could we be an example? Although this danger is not immediate, Americans seem to be preparing themselves against the prospect that what Jefferson called the "Empire for Liberty" should be bounded only by the earth. Our children, already equipped with supersonic space-ships, are getting ready to make Mars safe for democracy.

7. PATHS TO NATIONAL SELF-DISCOVERY: U.S.A. AND PUERTO RICO

To deprive a people of their traditional rights will stir them to indignation and action. But to deprive them of their traditional grievances may also impose a sense of frustration and a loss of bearings. American history gives us examples of both kinds of discontent.

Before the American Revolution, the people of the Thirteen Colonies were stirred to anger by violation of what they conceived to be their traditional rights as Englishmen. But they did have the satisfaction of being able to blame their economic and political ills (some of which actually had come from bad weather or hostile Indians) on the wicked machinations of a mad King, his Machiavellian ministers, and an irresponsible Parliament. One of the frustrations under which some leading American Revolutionaries (like Sam Adams and Patrick Henry) suffered in the years following separation from Great Britain was that they had deprived themselves of their oppressor. Their grievances had held them precariously together during the war and had given them their political bearings for at least a decade. Now they had to discover, without assistance from George III and his ministers, what it meant to be American.

One of the best examples of the kind of frustration we suffered in those early years is found in Puerto Rico. For the Puerto Ricans, too, have suffered both the discontent of oppression and the discontent of liberation. From the American occupation of the island in 1898 until recently its inhabitants had few powers of self-government, but the novel legal arrangement which in 1952 created the Commonwealth of Puerto Rico has given the island an almost uninhibited control over its internal affairs. This fact, apparent to common sense, was actually certified by the General Assembly of the United Nations (November 27, 1953) when it resolved that Puerto Rico was no longer to be classified as a non-self-governing or "dependent" area. Created outside familiar molds, the new formula of a "Free Associated State" (*Estado Libre Asociado*) has sought to satisfy insular demands for autonomy without breaking the bond with the United States. By removing many of the traditional political grievances of the island, the Commonwealth "settlement" has, of course, required a radical revision of the traditional Puerto Rican image of the United States. Yet it was in that very image that Puerto Ricans had long found their main clue to what they were in themselves. One result has been a vague but growing malaise among the intellectuals of the island.

This is only another case of the unhappiness suffered by a people suddenly deprived of their ancient grievances. Take the Irish since the creation of the Free State. Or consider those Jews who, because they find anti-Semitism an obstacle to self-fulfillment, become Zionists. Having settled in Israel, where *ex hypothesi* anti-Semitism cannot exist, they sometimes feel as much frustrated as fulfilled. They discover only then how heavily they have leaned on the fact (and their belief in the fact) of discrimination.

Much more than the American colonials before the Revolution, Puerto Ricans over the past two centuries had taken their intellectual bearings from their relationship to their oppressors (real or supposed). Even today each of the three principal Puerto Rican political parties must be distinguished primarily by its stand on the question of the proper status of Puerto Rico in relation to the United States. The preoccupation with this problem is much deeper than the casual observer would guess. It is no exaggeration to say that nearly all the major writers and thinkers of Puerto Rico have been concerned with the question of "status"— that is, of the proper relationship between the island and its "mother" country. Before 1898 the question was oriented toward Spain; afterwards, toward the United States. Most of the intellectual heritage of Puerto Rico, then, consists of a miscellany of polemics, legal essays, political oratory, poetry, reminiscence, and threnody, all centering on the theme of status.

We can begin to understand what this means for the intellectual life of a community if we imagine that the American Revolution for some reason or other had not happened, and American politics had continued for nearly two centuries to be a debate on the limited issue of parliamentary jurisdiction over taxation. In that case, on the continent today, we would still have a party of "Internal Taxationists," a party of "External Taxationists" (believing that Parliament could tax only the external commerce of the colonies), a "Dominion" party, and an "Independence" party. Such has been the framework of Puerto Rican politics.

But, as everybody knows, the course of American colonial debate broadened between 1765 and 1776; from the feasibility, legality, or justice of a particular law to the largest constitutional questions. This meant that although the Revolution did, of course, mark a decisive break in the legal relations between the American colonies and Great Britain, there was no significant discontinuity in American political thought. Many of the questions which had concerned Franklin and Jefferson and Pendleton and John Adams during the Revolution continued to be debated in the Constitutional Convention of 1787, persisted into the Republican-Federalist controversies of the early years of the new nation, and actually became central issues in the Civil War. Some would say that these are still the topics on which Democrats and Republicans disagree. The American Revolution was thus a seminal event: the intellectual preliminaries to the Revolution provided an ample (but not too large or too vague) arena of political debate for decades to come.

The thinking of Puerto Rican statesmen and intellectuals, however, never broadened out fruitfully from the specific question of status to the nature of constitutions and federations as American thought did between about 1760 and 1787. It it hard to read the chief figures in Puerto Rican political thought—men like Muñoz Rivera and Pedreira—without being struck by how little they have had to say about the large issues of political theory. They have not inquired broadly into the social compact, the character of federalism, or the nature of human rights; nor (with the possible exception of de Hostos) have they contributed significantly to either Spanish or American constitutional history. Overwhelmingly preoccupied with Puerto Rican status, they had failed to put it in a broad framework. For that reason, the creation of the Commonwealth of 1952 (which removed many of the causes of the status grievances) dissolved much of the traditional subject matter of their political thought.

I.

By its very espousal of the settlement of 1952, the Popular Democratic Party led by the able Governor Muñoz Marin, has indicated its unwillingness to walk the timeworn path of Puerto Rican political thought any longer, though not by actually abandoning the status issue. The Governor's party still contains many members of independentist sentiment; and the party has retained the traditionally sharp focus and limited view of Puerto Rican politics, but has made them a virtue by now focusing on problems that most affect the standard of living.

Meanwhile, the two minority parties (the Independentists and the Republicans or Statists), which between them in recent elections have won only about 35 per cent of the popular vote, have remained heirs of the traditional preoccupation of insular politics. This would raise problems for any political leader, and especially for one as sensitive as the Governor. It is not surprising then that he has recently had a part in translating the status issue from political to cultural terms. According to the Governor's own professions, the political relations of the island to the United States will not for a long time require basic revision of the Commonwealth compact. His welfare and development programs presuppose its preservation. Yet, as the Governor carefully points out, industrial progress and assimilation to the United States create a new problem of *cultural* status.

Governor Luis Muñoz Marin is a remarkable combination of poet and pragmatist. What distinguishes him among world political leaders today—and qualifies him as a kind of Winston Churchill of the Caribbean—is that he possesses a feeling both for those ineffable traditional elements which must be expressed poetically and for those everyday needs of a people which can be added up in dollars and cents. To him, status as a political issue has for some years been decreasing in interest; it lacks both spiritual suggestiveness and practical utility. In 1936, when he had been expelled from the Puerto Rican Liberal Party for his independentist views, he retired from politics to country life for two years or so. He learned then from the *jíbaros* among whom he lived that the ordinary Puerto Rican, while indifferent to the hackneyed issue of political status, was intensely interested in social and economic welfare. Since then Muñoz Marin has risen politically by slogans and programs of social improvement.

At the same time, the Governor is genuinely concerned with the problem of what it really means to be a Puerto Rican. Social and economic changes dramatize the problem. These are, for the most part, consequences of industrialization, which for this island has meant Americanization. Many of the rising middle class in San Juan live in replicas of Miami suburbs, like Baldrich, Caparra Heights, or Garden Hills. The visitor to one of these suburbs is greeted by a sign announcing the place of the weekly meeting of the local Rotary Club and another (auspices of the Lion's Club) requesting: "Drive Slow: We Love Our Children." Properly qualified residents may join a continental type of country club. They equip their houses with deep-freezers, "hi-fi," air-conditioning, and television sets on which the family watches Lucille Ball and Desi Arnaz weekly. An impressive number of Cadillacs in salmon, pink, and mauve prove the species acclimated to the tropics. English is, of course, the lingua franca. If a continental visitor tries to compliment a resident by speaking halting Spanish, this is likely to be taken as a criticism of the listener's English and hence of his social status. In such neighborhoods, only the servants do not speak English. The magazines on living room coffee-tables include *Time, Better Homes and Gardens, The Saturday Evening Post,* and *Mademoiselle* (all in English).

The Governor, who is both thoroughly American and thoroughly Puerto Rican, exemplifies a harmonious cultural dualism. Yet his own rise to power is a symbol of Puerto Rican autonomy, a kind of fulfillment of the Puerto Rican personality. Can he then be blamed if he is disturbed to see Puerto Ricans improving themselves in so un-Puerto Rican a fashion? What, he wonders, are Puerto Ricans in and for themselves? He seeks desperately for some native flavor, some power of resistance, to prevent the island from becoming a mere receptacle of imported culture.

But what are the resources out of which a native character can be built in Puerto Rico? From the commonplaces of modern history one can list some factors which have often helped communities toward a pungent and vigorous national character. These would include: (1) *geographic smallness* (or natural boundaries), illustrated by the British, the Dutch, or the Swiss; (2) *a characteristic landscape* (preferably distinctive from that of its near neighbors), illustrated by the insularity of England, the mountainousness of Switzerland, the wateriness of the Netherlands; (3) *a rich or characteristic history,* illustrated by the wealth of drama and episode of the Italian city-states, or the colorful but unidirectional character of the history of the United States; (4) *long membership in a community of nations,* illustrated by the Scandinavian countries, or parts of the British Commonwealth.

Puerto Rico possesses none of these gratuitous aids to communal self-discovery, with the exception of geographic smallness. The geographic and climatic sameness of the Antilles has cursed all these islands in their quests for separate identities. Where insularity is universal, no one community has a distinctive advantage in being an island. Perhaps nowhere else in the world are neighboring political communities so uncomplementary from an economic or cultural point of view. They have the same crops; someone has said that they have nothing to export to each other but their diseases. It would be hard to find any other region where geographic neighbors seem so remote; for they see each other not directly but in the distant mirrors of New York, London, Paris, and Amsterdam.

In the days of the buccaneers, Puerto Rico and

its neighbors were a natural community of mutual warfare and exploitation; in pre-Columbian days they were probably ranged over by the same Indian tribes. But in recent centuries an unfortunate set of circumstances has deprived Puerto Rico of its natural neighbors—and, incidentally, of those aids to self-discovery which many nations find in nearby communities with which they can compare themselves. Puerto Rico lacks the predominantly Negro population of its Caribbean neighbors; this has deprived it of the sense of racial reawakening which has inspired Negroes in some other parts of the world. Brute facts, then, would seem to support the pessimism of the nineteenth-century Spanish writer who described Puerto Rico as "the corpse of a society that has never been born."

This bitter comment is, of course, a slander on the vital spirit of contemporary Puerto Rico. Even one who visits there briefly cannot fail to sense the quickening of social and economic life. But the nineteenth-century slander could still be paraphrased to describe accurately the considerable number of Puerto Rican intellectuals who, with blind highfalutin enthusiasm, seek "rebirth" of a culture which was never born a first time. Of course, literary people everywhere prefer what has been made accessible in the neat pages of books and in works of art to the whirr of life around them. In Puerto Rico these days they therefore try to re-create their past in the familiar image of the rich cultures of Europe.

Through the Ateneo (Puerto Rico's academy of arts and letters), the daily newspapers, and in many other ways, they seek to "discover" ("invent" would be more accurate) a Puerto Rican High

Culture, complete with poets, novelists, historians, dramatists, philosophers, and painters. By collecting *santos* (small religious images carved of wood or modeled in plaster by amateur artists for domestic use), by romanticizing the image of the *jibaro,* and by stimulating textile and pottery crafts, they also try to conjure up a rich Folk Culture. In the long run, the results of this double effort are not likely to fool anyone. They will not convince either Puerto Ricans or others that the island possesses a character of its own.

In order to make the most of their natural charms, the people of Puerto Rico must first discover, confront, and even embrace their limitations.

In no area is this more important than in relation to their past. Yet here, least of all, have Puerto Rican intellectuals been willing to face the crude facts. An academic traveler to the island cannot help being startled by the assumption (more accurately described as an article of patriotic faith) that Puerto Rico possesses a "glorious past"—or at least a history vastly rich, interesting, and instructive. Among the literary class one often hears the lament that there has never been an artistically first-rate, scholarly, and comprehensive History of Puerto Rico. This has even been made into a kind of accusation, which by its self-evidence is supposed to clinch the argument, against the University of Puerto Rico. Meanwhile in the University itself one finds among historians an almost pathological preoccupation with the history of Puerto Rico, which has become one of the most flourishing academic industries on the island. An extensive course in the history of Puerto Rico is required in many parts of the University, and draws one of the largest enrollments. Nearly all the senior members of the History Department are "specialists" in one aspect or another of the history of Puerto Rico. Yet critics of the University lament its inattention to the local past; and professors promise to do still more with Puerto Rican history in the future.

This communal myopia comes from a simple unquestioned assumption. Because the English, the French, and the Spanish have found a flattering mirror of national character in their epic past, Puerto Ricans (who *ex hypothesi* have a national character) also must have such a mirror. But in their fervor to make themselves interesting by inflating their past, Puerto Ricans have been inclined to overlook (or even deny) some of their peculiarities that may actually be advantages.

One of the more obvious of these is that Puerto Rico is a country with a long past but a short history. Any historian who studies the Puerto Rican past as a narrative of men and institutions comparable to those of France, England, Holland, Japan, or Israel, cannot honestly claim it to be particularly eventful. Puerto Rico's political history lacks even a single revolution or civil war of intense drama or of decisive significance. Its cultural history has produced few monuments (with the notable exception of the fortress El Morro). Its institutional history has produced few striking phenomena. Some explanations are, of course, obvious. Because Puerto Rico was long a colony most of its history took place in Madrid, London, or Washington. The smallness and geographic homogeneity of the island have meant that it has lacked the internal dramatic conflict found in larger, more varied communities. Its insularity has preserved it from that ebb and flow across borders which has enriched the history of continental nations.

The seductive fact is that despite its spectacularly thin history, Puerto Rico has (at least from a European point of view) one of the longest pasts of any part of the New World. Columbus landed there; San Juan was a European settlement in the early sixteenth century. In this paradox lies the danger that Puerto Ricans should be tempted to expect too much of their history, by hastily concluding from its chronological extent that they can find in it the same resource which some other communities have found. England, France, and Italy, for example, have both impressively long and impressively rich histories; the United States, a rich and eventful history crammed into a short span of years but spread thinly over a large geographic extent. Many other parts of the world, like India and China, had a wealth of history before they were seen by European eyes. But the Puerto Rican people are married to a thinly historied landscape. They would do better to discover the peculiar virtues of that landscape rather than lust after charms not legitimately theirs.

Some of these advantages will appear in bold relief against the life of another, much larger community which, like Puerto Rico, suffers both from overpopulation and from a lack of natural resources. Italy suffers not only from these ills, but also from a feeling of contemporary inadequacy, from a rigidity in approaching its social problems, and from an excessively ideological politics—all of which are related to its embarrassingly rich history. Where can one match the cultural inheritance of the Italians, from ancient Etruscan through Roman, medieval, papal, and Renaissance to liberal-modern? This wealth has, of course, helped the Italians to think well of themselves. But it has had its temptations: Mussolini strutted in the toga of Caesar. Even today many Italians grope aimlessly in the shadows of their own great past. While that past is a magnificent many-chambered palace ready-made for all later generations, it can also be a many-celled prison. The very monuments which make Italy the world's greatest museum tempt the living Italian to overwhelming and obsolete standards of self-judgment. Nowadays the Italians are inclined to run the gamut of old solutions for new problems, or to assume that problems are insoluble. But the times call for a liberated imagination.

Anyone who goes from Italy to Puerto Rico can hardly fail to see that the island's lack of history may be a natural asset. Unencumbered by the baggage of a magnificent past, Puerto Ricans can discover grandeur in improving the present. And without that resentment characteristic of nations emerged from destructive revolutions or who have known better times, they can open their windows to the future.

If we turn from the general orientation of the life of the community to the vocabulary of politics, we find similar fortuitous advantages in the actual Puerto Rican situation. That imprisonment of Puerto Rican political thought within the issue of status, which we have already remarked, has, of course, been itself a symptom of the thinness of Puerto Rican history. If the island had had its full share of turbulent idealism, *coups d'état,* bloody revolutions, destructive civil wars, ruthless foreign invasions (and the other familiar chapters in the history of European nations), it might have acquired a more grandiose and metaphysical political vocabulary. The antithesis with Italy is again illuminating, because in this respect too, Puerto Rico and Italy are polar opposites. Italian politics is a morass of ideology. You have no trouble in getting an Italian politician or university student to describe the Good Society: he talks in beautiful abstractions, while he points to remotely glittering pinnacles. But he is reticent or indifferent about those myriad details (tariff, social security, taxation, etc.) which are the daily life of a people. How different is Puerto Rico! Here politicians are nothing if not specific. Recently the Popular Democratic Party has focused political debate on the most concrete social and economic questions: social security, industrialization, literacy, disease, and nutrition. Even the minority parties are oriented around limited objectives: the Republican (or Statist) Party favoring statehood within the United States, and the Independentist Party seeking political independence.

If the status issue has been a prison keeping Puerto Rican political thinkers from the invigorating winds of doctrine blowing outside, it has also protected them from the windiness of political metaphysics and metaphysical politicians. Today Puerto Rico is reaping unexpected benefits from the failure of its earlier political thinkers to enter the boundless arena of philosophic speculation. It is no small advantage nowadays that the Puerto Rican politician is in the habit of thinking specifically, even if sometimes he has been inclined to think pettily. Contemporary Puerto Rican politics is a refreshing spectacle of people grappling with their major problems. One must look hard and long on the island to find anyone enchanted by the mirages of fascism, communism, monarchism, socialism, or the ideal of a Christian Society. On the continent of Europe these days, the contrary is the case; there even democracy has lost its flavor of compromise and become a kind of castle in the air. Italian or French political parties are the awkward effort to continue numerous uncompleted revolutions within the framework of peaceful political life. But in Puerto Rico, with its relatively barren political past, the leading statesmen find nothing more interesting than the present—unless it be the future.

II.

The main obstacle encountered by a community like Puerto Rico in its quest for a self-respecting and distinctive character is its tendency to judge itself by abstract and absolute standards. This is, of course, the common paradox of modern nationalism: nations self-consciously in search of their souls often try to model themselves after a chimera bred of past "great cultures." But the great resource of community self-respect is not the large noble aspiration; it is rather the specific and distinctive fact. For a people to discover the utility of one of its natural limitations is worth a dozen patriotic hymns.

The advantages of this approach appear nowhere more clearly than in the case of Puerto Rico. For if it is poor in the familiar repertoire of European nations, it can have a small and respectable repertoire all its own. I shall try to give a hint of how some features of contemporary Puerto Rican life might be viewed not as obstacles to its assimilation to the pattern of "great nations" but as possibly unique opportunities. The list could be indefinitely extended; my items are meant only to be suggestive.

Bilingualism

Everywhere in Puerto Rico one hears about "the language problem." The double claims of two languages have burdened many Puerto Ricans, especially those who suffered for many years under the legal requirement that English be the first language of the schools. Some Puerto Ricans who barely knew English were forced to learn arithmetic, geography, and science through it; they are understandably resentful. Only recently the Governor expressed his fear that the pressure to learn two languages had made islanders not bilingual but "semi-lingual in two languages." This is "the language problem." But this Puerto Rican situation can be viewed in another light. The visitor to the island is struck by the remarkable bilingualism of the Puerto Rican middle classes; at the University of Puerto Rico, for example, the native faculty speak both Spanish and English. The Puerto Rican middle classes are amazingly competent at making themselves understood in idiomatic English. Perhaps nowhere else in the Americas, and in few parts of Europe, are so large a proportion of the leading classes so much at home in two languages. This offers a novel opportunity, although Puerto Rican nationalists persist in seeing it almost exclusively as a problem.

The canons of abstract and imitative nationalism

do, of course, require that every nation have its own "pure" language. Recently the Philippines have made trouble for themselves by adopting Tagalog to prove their national identity. Fortunately Puerto Rico possesses no surviving native tongue. But *their* language is presumably Spanish, just as for the Irish Free State it is Gaelic and for Israel, Hebrew. The futile aspiration to linguistic purism has been encouraged by the Governor, for example, in his speech (December 29, 1953) to the association of schoolteachers, which attacked the current "corruption" of the Spanish language. A sign, "Agapito's Bar," which he encountered in a remote Puerto Rican town, he made symbolic of the growing willingness to slouch into English words instead of sticking with pure Spanish. "Language is the breath of the spirit. Let's not allow our breathing to become asthmatic," he pled. "With asthma, we can't ascend the heights." The Puerto Rican Academy for the Spanish Language (headed by the president of the insular senate) has undertaken a program to preserve the purity of the mother tongue.

Meanwhile, literate Puerto Ricans are being sought out for important jobs throughout Latin America—not because they speak literary Spanish or literary English, but because they have a unique idiomatic command of the two. Is it not a rare good chance that so small an island with so little history and literature of its own, should be blessed with linguistic avenues to so much of the rest of the world? Why should Puerto Ricans lament that they cannot make language the vehicle of a "pure" literature when they are peculiarly well situated to put it to other uses?

The Extended Kinship Family

The high rate of population growth is, of course, one of the main obstacles to the rapid economic improvement of the island. An important element in encouraging the production of numerous children is the special character of the Puerto Rican family. This is what sociologists call the "extended kinship family," based on the strength of the blood tie, and on the idea that one man has a claim on another simply because he is his relative. With every additional child a parent adds capital (which may be compounded) to provide for his old age. Consequences of this institution are far-reaching and cannot be expressed only in population statistics. For some time there has been a growing tendency on the island to emphasize only its evils. Meanwhile, the "Fomento" program of industrial development and the recent emigration to the continent have increased mobility, and have made it harder for the old-fashioned family to survive.

There are, however, several characteristic virtues in the traditional Puerto Rican family. Most important, perhaps, it provides the child with a sense of belonging (as one of the ablest students of the Puerto Rican family has observed); he is valued for *who* he is rather than for *what* he is. The members of the old kinship group were valued with little regard to their special talents and worldly promise; membership was the important thing. Perhaps this failed to provide strong pressures to worldly success. But it nourished a characteristically democratic attitude: whether halt, blind, rich, poor, bright, or stupid, every person was valued simply because he was himself. The kinship family thus has helped inoculate the people of the island against some of the worst excesses of a survival-of-the-fittest industrial philosophy. In a community which has never been rich and must face a meager economy for decades to come, the feeling of personal security, dignity, and innate worth fostered by this institution can be invaluable. It is probably this institution that makes real the notions of *serenidad* and *dignidad* so often eulogized by Puerto Rican patriots. Perhaps, too, the courtesy and generosity which the stranger encounters in Puerto Rico are somehow connected with the willingness of people to extend their kin-patterns to a larger circle of neighbors and visitors.

The Position of Women in Public Life

Among the more interesting examples of self-disparagement, of the readiness of the islanders to cast their virtues in an alien mold, is their attitude toward the position of women. Anyone who goes to the island from the continental United States cannot fail to be struck by the number of remarkable women in its public life. In 1955, for example, there were Doña Felisa Rincón de Gautier (the effective mayoress of San Juan) and four other mayoresses out of an insular total of 76, two lady senators (out of 32) and two representatives (out of 64). The president of the Ateneo has been the vivid Señorita Nilita Vientós Gastón; and there is an impressively numerous female faculty at the University of Puerto Rico. These women seem more successful in preserving their attractive femininity than many of their counterparts in the continental

United States. The leading ladies of Puerto Rican public life play a distinctively different role from that of the American "career woman."

Still they like to put themselves in the tradition of Mary Wollstonecraft, John Stuart Mill, and the American suffragettes. European liberalism, they say, has everywhere (as in Puerto Rico) carried belief in the equality of women. But may not the place held by women in the public life of the island be somehow related to characteristics of the local family and kinship institutions? Perhaps the "equality" of Puerto Rican women is less analogous to that espoused by Western liberalism, than to that of the women of India. Perhaps the Puerto Rican—like the Hindu—family has long provided within itself a kind of challenging, extensive, and responsible managerial role for the wife which is easily translated into a larger community. May not Puerto Rico then have a unique opportunity to preserve many values of an ancient family organization within the novel contexts of democracy and industrialization?

Political Institutions in a Puerto Rican Style

Commonwealth status is, of course, an inspired example of success in providing new solutions for new problems. But without intending it, and perhaps without wanting it, the island has produced other striking political novelties. Take, for example, the particular approach to planning. Perhaps nothing is more misleading than the frequent reference to contemporary Puerto Rican politics as a perpetuation of the New Deal. In the continental United States we have long taken it for granted that no part of the economy should be planned by the government without some special justification like national defense or economic emergency. We have strong historical justification for our attitude: the free play of self-interest and private enterprise on our fantastically rich continent has helped produce unprecedented levels of human welfare and industrial progress.

But the people of Puerto Rico have had much less reason to put their faith in the free play of private ambition. In a country where "striking it rich" has been a myth (except in the government lottery) and where every thirty years or so whimsically destructive hurricanes demolish houses and crops, people are more receptive to the advantages of planning. At the same time, doctrinaire socialist approaches to planning, as to other political problems, have had very little appeal. At first the Socialist Party of the island had a vaguely Marxist flavor, but during most of its never very successful life its leaders were preoccupied with the status issue. The party has now for all practical purposes ceased to exist, because its gubernatorial candidate in 1952 polled only three per cent of the ten per cent required of a party to retain its legal standing. The present government is neither socialist nor antisocialist; it has simply shown a refreshing readiness to plan or not to plan as the occasion has required. It has been willing to try government ownership in limited cases where it seemed temporarily necessary; but it has been equally willing to abandon experiments in government ownership when they no longer seem desirable. In Puerto Rico, then, planning is viewed neither as an emergency deviation from a *laissez-faire* orthodoxy, nor as an orthodoxy in itself, but simply as one political expedient among many others. The resulting program has a distinctive flavor.

The United States as a Puerto Rican Frontier: and Vice Versa

Puerto Rico remains one of the few areas from which people can freely immigrate to the United States. This not only provides a frontier of economic opportunity, an outlet for population and energy, but it can also have (and is already having) a broad effect on the island itself, giving it the advantage of free intercourse with a larger, more advanced community, while retaining many of the advantages of smallness and insularity. Paradoxically the United States has become a kind of "colony" of Puerto Rico, not only as an outlet for its surplus population, but as a source of raw materials for many of the new industries of the island. This, together with the more familiar fact that Puerto Rico is a "frontier" for continental capital (and population), puts the island in the novel situation of simultaneously possessing advantages both of being a "colony" and of being a "mother country."

In Puerto Rico there is a growing communal self-consciousness, an impulse to self-discovery. It sometimes seems a kind of adolescent *Weltschmerz*. There, as elsewhere, the literary classes possess a terrible power to impose on the community an aimless malaise. But if they can guide the island to self-definition along empirical, particularist lines they can prevent the vagrant quest for the self, based on false parallels with other countries and on borrowed standards of self-realization. That quest is bound to be sterile and to add needless frustration to an already insecure community. Their proper role is to help the community find itself, not by leading a strenuous quest of Culture, but by helping their countrymen to discover and develop those social resources which are indigenous to the country.

8. A DIALOGUE OF TWO HISTORIES: JEWISH AND AMERICAN

No problem is more American than how to make "one" culture out of many. Each group—racial, national, or religious—that has come to this country has, of course, brought distinctive elements from remote places and distant pasts. But the influence of England and Western Europe, of Protestant institutions and Caucasian peoples, has obviously been dominant. And this simple fact has always troubled us whenever we try to place all the other influences. Unifying our national culture is usually described as the problem of how to "fit in" all the non-European, non-Caucasian, non-Protestant elements. We had Japanese resettlement camps during the Second World War (though there had been no comparable camps for Germans in either of the World Wars), and before that our Chinese Exclusion Acts. In states where the Negro population equals that of the Whites, we persist in speaking of the "Negro Problem"—though anyone looking at the facts might better describe it as the "White Problem." Our general assumption has long been that people who do not come from West European, White, Protestant stock are somehow unassimilable: somehow indelibly "un-American." This extends even to New World peoples, as exemplified in our attitude toward American Indians, Mexicans, and Puerto Ricans. We can still seriously discuss whether a Catholic "ought" to be President of the United States, although Catholics comprise by far the largest religious sect in the country.

These prevailing assumptions have themselves become part of our problem. Every "normal" American must make up his mind about "minority groups," he must "decide what he thinks" about Negroes, Jews, Catholics, Mexicans, Puerto Ricans, and Japanese. The "minorities" themselves are burdened with defining their relation to the American main stream. But general theories of American culture and of the American Way of Life are not very helpful. Each group must ask itself different questions. The Negro-Americans, for example, who are primarily racially defined, obviously face problems very different from those of German-Americans, Polish-Americans, or Italian-Americans, who are defined by national and linguistic background. The Catholics, defined by a religious tradition, have other problems; and the problems of Irish-Catholics are again different from those of Italian- or Polish-Catholics. And the Jews, who somehow combine all these (and other) peculiarities, have still others.

Yet much of what each of these groups has said about itself is actually not concerned with the tantalizingly complex and fruitful relations among our many American cultures, but is simply aimed to refute the popular assumption that it is "un-American." They are concerned less with self-discovery than with self-defense. Much of what they write is a simple-minded brief against a vague indictment for un-Americanism—rather than a description of what they themselves promise for America.

This defense usually takes one of two forms. First, an effort to show that the particular group—even *before* it came to America—had fervently espoused true Americanism. This is a kind of prenatal Americanism, a claim to have been American even before America was born. We read accounts of the long tradition of liberal democracy in Germany and Italy; and arguments that the "main stream" of Catholicism (expressed in the great Catholic political theorists like Thomas Aquinas and Suarez) has always in spirit been essentially tolerant and democratic. Or that the Jews, ever since the Exodus from Egypt, have been "fighters for freedom" and that in all the centuries when they were celebrating the Passover Seder they were really anticipating the Fourth of July.

Second, the effort to show that the group has already contributed here a great deal that is "typically American." This is an *ex post facto* Americanism: the claim that what was actually the product of sometimes unhappy historical and geographic coincidences must instead be looked on as the fulfillment of a special talent to enrich American culture. Thus Negroes make much of spirituals and of jazz. Jews and Catholics prove their importance as financiers and fighters of the American Revolution and the Civil War. The "Americanism" of Negroes and Puerto Ricans is confirmed by their contributions to big-league baseball.

I doubt whether arguments like these ever prove much. At best they are antidefamation propaganda; primarily they solace the people who have been defamed. They can never reveal to us the peculiarly fertile relation among cultures which has been possible in the United States. Yet this is what we should be thinking about. Instead of defending ourselves against chauvinists by becoming chauvinists ourselves, we might better try to discover some of the peculiarly "un-American" vitamins that each of us may add to the skimmed milk of Caucasian-English-West-European-Protestantism.

The case of the American Jews illustrates all these common problems and also how subtly different is the problem of each group. The Jewish inheritance includes some distinctively racial, some distinctively national, and some distinctively religious elements. And Jewish spokesmen, haunted by the specter of anti-Semitism, have been especially preoccupied with "defense." They have seemed more anxious to prove the Jewish title to a share in authentically American culture than to discover how they are qualified to enrich it. Like other American religious sects, they too have given in to the temptation to equate the special tenets of their religion with "real" Americanism. Yet the capacity of Jews to contribute to American civilization is by no means proportionate to the affinity of traditional Judaism with orthodox Americanism. Here least of all can we look for harmonious dogmas: Judaism is one of the least dogmatic of religions, and American orthodoxy is a myth.

A fertile encounter between Jewish and American culture may perhaps best be defined historically. We must not seek the tenets of any dominant creed; we must look rather for what is characteristic of each of two historical experiences. We must be willing to face their true diversity, and even to make that diversity the measure of what the two have to say to each other. Cultures, we must remember, are not characterized by dogmas, but by assumptions or emphases; not by creeds to be defended, but by possibilities to be explored. They are more like responsive personalities than consistent systems of thought. Inevitably, their relationship will contain tensions; to be a living relationship it must contain tensions. Among cultures it is often the marriage of opposites that is the happiest and the most fruitful.

If we examine the large features of the Jewish, as distinguished from the American, historical experience, I believe we will discover the materials for just such a dynamic tension. The dramatic contrast between the two will not only help us discover the kind of dialogue which can exist between our two experiences and traditions, but may even help us define the mission of Jews on this continent. The American and the Jewish historical experiences, we will find, differ at least with respect to dimension, arena, and orientation.

The difference of chronological *dimension* is perhaps the most obvious. While the American is the most precocious of living Western cultures, the Jewish is the most venerable. The history of culture in the United States extends over a period of three hundred years at the most; Jewish history (even if dated only from the departure from Egypt circa 1445 B.C.) is at least ten times that long. The whole of American history could be confined in the chronological boundaries of a single chapter of Jewish history. The period from the age of Hillel to the writing down of the Babylonian Talmud is approximately twice the length of all American history.

A result has been a striking difference of attitude toward time: in this the Jewish and the American views have been polar opposites. The brevity of the American past has led to a failure to give due importance to the whole human inheritance, and to a readiness to attach disproportionate importance to any one man or generation. "The American is a new man, who acts upon new principles," boasted Crèvecoeur in the era of the Revolution, "he must therefore entertain new ideas, and form new opinions." In a Brave New World Americans have been eager to see man in heroic nakedness. And man stripped of his institutional and traditional inheritance seems a mere biological creature. The classic formulation of this emphasis in political theory is found in Jeffersonian political thought, resting as it does on a materialist anthropology, defending the equality of men by their common membership in the species *homo sapiens,* and maintaining the superiority of political life in America because this continent lacks an institutional past.

What has seemed to characterize man in America has not been his new American garments so much as his new opportunity to see his unadorned beauty. In Whitman's words we hear a theme which reappears in many unexpected places in American culture, from Jefferson and Jackson through Theodore Roosevelt, John Dewey, and Ruth Benedict.

I sing the body electric. . . .
The swimmer naked in the swimming-bath, seen as he
    swims through the transparent green-shine, or lies
    with his face up and rolls silently to and fro in the
    heave of the water. . . .

The wrestle of wrestlers, two apprentice boys, quite
grown, lusty, good-natured, native-born, out on the
vacant lot at sundown after work. . . .
The march of firemen in their own costumes, the play
of masculine muscle through clean-setting trowsers
and waist-straps. . . .
Swim with the swimmers, wrestle with wrestlers, march
in line with the firemen, and pause, listen, count.
O my body! I dare not desert the likes of you in other
men and women, nor the likes of the parts of you.

But the Jew, least of all men, can believe in the
nakedness of man: the past is forced on him—if
not inwardly, at least by society. Perforce he has a
historical orientation. Even his God (as the Rabbi
in Halevi's *Kuzari* insisted) is a historical figure,
identified by actual past accomplishments, "the God
of Abraham, Isaac, and Jacob, who brought our
fathers forth from the land of bondage." The Bible
of Judaism is replete with begats and the careers
of generations.

In America, of all commodities the most precious
has been *time*. It has been one of the few strikingly
scarce commodities in our national history. Colonial
history was a race among European nations for
control of the continent; recent American history
has been a race among individuals and corporations
for a continent's treasure. Nor is it surprising that
Americans should be impatient; since time does
not stretch back endlessly into the national past, it
seems unlikely to stretch endlessly into the future.
But for the Jew time has been abundant. In Veb-
len's phrase, the Jewish mind bears the date-mark
B.C. According to the familiar story, when Bismarck
confronted the French with his bill for reparations

after the Franco-Prussian War, they complained that to pay such an amount would take them more years than had elapsed since the birth of Jesus. Bismarck replied (pointing to the Jew Gerson Bleichröder), that that was why he had brought with him a man whose people started their calendar not from the birth of Jesus, but from the creation of the world.

The disparity of chronological dimension has contributed to a difference of attitude toward the intelligibility of history, if not of all experience. The beginning of the United States—not so many decades ago—is a story rich in facts: we know by name and even by portrait many of the earliest settlers, and when and why they came here. Our republic was formed at a precise and historical period. The destination of American history has appeared equally plain, for optimism and a belief in progress have made the present age seem to us (as it did to John Winthrop, Benjamin Franklin, and Calvin Coolidge) the culmination of the past. The peculiar American version of destiny has been *"manifest destiny,"* with clarity its hallmark. The American past contains few, if any, mythical characters.

American history could then be described as "closed" at both ends: both origin and destination appear fixed. In contrast Jewish history is open at both ends. The creation of the Jewish people is shrouded in twilight; the mystery of Jewish destiny has been its authentic stamp. God made the beginning and the end, and only His back are we permitted to see. The creation of the world merges indefinitely into the creation of the Law and the mystery of truth.

The Lord made me as the beginning of His way,
The first of His works of old.
I was set up from everlasting, from the beginning,
Or ever the earth was.
When there were no depths, I was brought forth;
When there were no fountains abounding with
   water. . . .
Then I was by Him, as a nursling;
And I was daily all delight,
Playing always before Him,
Playing in His habitable earth,
And my delights are with the sons of men.

(Proverbs, 8:22 ff.)

The mystery of the Beginning is paralleled by the mystery of the End, expressed in a Messiah who is certain to come, is always about to come, yet whose coming is always in the future.

To see history *sub specie Americani* is to be encouraged in an excessive (if well substantiated) optimism. Jews, viewing history *sub specie aeternitatis,* incline to pessimism, however much tinged by Zionistic utopianism. For Americans, America *is* Zion; but for Jews even the achievement of a Jewish state does not make Zion attained.

In the *arena* of historical experience we find a contrast no less dramatic: the characteristic arena of American history has been *nature,* while that of Jewish history has been *society*. The epic of American history is the conquest of a continent, unprecedented in rapidity and thoroughness. It is a tale of Man against Nature. Crossing mountain ranges, irrigating deserts, digging gold and silver, discovering and extracting oil, cutting down forests

—such achievements have marked the history of the United States. We look in vain for works of this type in the history of the Jewish people, at least until the founding of Israel in the present generation. The crossing of the Red Sea is perhaps the last event of Jewish history of a peculiarly American grandeur, and even that was not accomplished by Jewish engineers.

But on a scale no less grand than that of American history, Jewish history has shown man in society. Its impressive accomplishment has been social: the survival and the actual development of a culture in the midst of peoples who have despised it. As American history has revealed with unique magnificence man's ability to adapt himself to varied physical environments and to exploit nature, Jewish history has revealed his potentialities for survival among other men, however different from him they may have been or have thought themselves to be. The Jewish experience has been the survival of a community among communities, in a Babylonian captivity or among the Marranos. It is understandable that American folk-heroes should be Daniel Boone, Davy Crockett, and Mike Fink, men clever with their hands, able to hew a forest, strangle a mountain lion or master a river, while Jewish folk-heroes are Moses, Elijah, and Judas Maccabaeus.

The emphasis on exploration and control of the natural environment has helped produce an American pre-eminence in technology which has its counterpart in the Jewish achievement in ethics. Public education in America has been preoccupied with *useful* knowledge; Jewish education (partly because so many avenues of usefulness have been closed to Jews, partly because of the nonnaturalistic temper of Jewish thought) has been interested in the eternal meaning of the Law. The urgent practical tasks of American civilization have made the convenient concept of law as an ethical minimum flourish here with unprecedented vigor. It has seemed particularly important that men be left free to do as they wish in every area not explicitly covered by the law. While this has nourished the libertarian tradition and a healthful disrespect of bureaucracy, it has also helped engender a bewildering multiplicity of statutes. At the opposite pole is the Jewish conception of every man's "legal" duty to *exceed* the demands of law.

The naturalistic arena has made American life conspicuously poor in ritual and has nourished an extraordinary directness and explicitness in approaching the problems of national life. While Jews have never ceased to seek a definition of a Jew (without ever expecting to find one), Americans for decades have been ready with oaths and pledges of allegiance, loyalty and sedition tests, and courses in citizenship supposed to make true Americans in short order. The very brevity of American history and the diversity of origin of Americans have required a doubly explicit reassurance of national identity. The Fourth of July has been celebrated by the Oration, in which a public figure exhorts his audience to loyalty and public virtue; the Passover (the analogous Jewish holiday) is marked by prayer, ritual, music, and symbol. The sermon, which has thus become secularized and acquired a prominent place in American political life, has played a small role in the Jewish religious experience.

In America, the pressure of physical problems

and the greatness of economic rewards, together with the variety of traditions which have sought to live together, have nourished a willingness—even an eagerness—to minimize differences of ideas. This has amounted often to a tendency to undervalue ideas themselves. Who would spend his energy on metaphysics with a virgin continent before him? As Benjamin Rush urged in the early nineteenth century, Americans dared not be so foolish as to turn their backs upon a gold mine in order to go chasing butterflies. But history has imposed on Jews an opposite necessity: having for centuries been denied ground to conquer, they have had to seek community through ideas.

If men coming to this continent have had nothing else, they have had land (at least until recently), and plenty of it, which they could call their own. In this sense the history of the United States has been perhaps more geographically defined than that of any other recent culture. What other nation could summarize its history by the movement of a line across a map? Nothing could be further from the character of Jewish history.

The difference of *orientation* between the American and the Jewish historical experiences is, of course, very much a result of those differences of dimension and of arena which we have already remarked. But it is in itself something quite fundamental. In American history man has for the most part *confronted* his enemy. European man comes to this continent and sweeps all before him; the frontier advances and the enemy is conquered. On the whole the American moves in one direction at a time, with his allies behind him and his enemies in front. Jewish history, however, has shown a people *surrounded* by its enemies. The difference may be summarized as that between an attitude of confrontation and one of encirclement. The American looks ahead toward the horizon. The Jew, with the walls of the ghetto or of the Gentiles around him, looks up to his God or down into himself or his community.

The American orientation has led to an emphasis on the simple and the measurable, and to a stunting of the sense of paradox and of that awareness of evil which goes with it. The American meets the dragon and kills him; he is confident that the dragon is then dead and he turns complacently to another battle. His is a statistical sort of dragon. Consider, for example, the American enthusiasm for legislation, and the belief in statutory panaceas, familiarly illustrated by the prohibition amendment, or by the fact that the "lawless" Western states from the beginning provided themselves with especially long and explicit constitutions. Mark Twain's *Life on the Mississippi* gives classic form to the struggle to master the River: a problem large and physical, but where the test of success is easy. The good man is the "square shooter" or the man who "plays according to the rules of the game." That the rules should be uncertain or the nature of the game itself mystifying, is not to be imagined. Not since the Puritans of early New England— who indeed had a Hebraic sense of encirclement by enemies—have we seen any considerable awareness of the problem of evil. Only in the present generation, with the invention of nuclear weapons, have Americans begun to rediscover the problem.

Finding his own survival itself a magnificent

paradox, the Jew has a feeling for paradox everywhere: "Better is one hour of repentance and good deeds in this world than the whole life of the world to come; yet better is one hour of blissfulness of spirit in the world to come than the whole life of this world" (*Pirke Aboth*). Jewish history amply documents a short-run pessimism and a long-run optimism; it is the perfect antidote for the naïveté which would believe any victory complete. Or which would repose confidently in the security of "unconditional surrender." The Jew does not underestimate the power of evil; he knows that the wicked cannot be counted.

Nowhere does the disparity appear in sharper relief than in a comparison of American and Jewish humor. American humor has for the most part been forthright, the humor of exaggeration, understatement, and rough-house—of the Tall Tale, Mark Twain, Mr. Dooley, Mack Sennett, and Will Rogers. But Jewish humor has been that of double-entendre, irony, paradox, and satire; its proper response is not the belly-laugh but the "tsk-tsk" and the nod of the head. In the world of Sholom Aleichem, where the Jew's afflictions prove his chosenness, the unexpected is normal.

The peculiarly American disposition to simplify, select, and digest has its counterpart in the Jewish disposition to expand and explore. The American willingness to reduce great mysteries to words of one syllable (to tell the life of Jesus in journalese and to advertise the Bible as "The World's Best Seller") is countered by the Jewish readiness to find in every syllable a world of mystery. If Jewish literature and folk-legends have been marked by monuments of expansion and commentary, the American public thrives on the short short story, on abridgments, pocket anthologies, and digests.

The straightforward orientation of American history has carried with it an emphasis on extension and quantity. Jefferson's dream was of a nation of one hundred million; to "populate" or "fill" the continent was a common aim of patriots of the early nineteenth century. Where else has the national census been so widely taken for an index of progress? But if the advance of civilization on this continent has seemed readily measurable in quantitative terms, the march of Jewish history has been least of all susceptible of such measurement. The Jew, lacking a continent to explore, has instead explored his mind and soul and his community. The decimation of the pogrom and the Nazi Gas Chamber make him least of all willing to measure his strength quantitatively. His aim has been not to extend, but to perfect; he has lived in a microcosm. His chief concerns have been with the manifold possibilities of the family, with the moral import of everyday life. His mission has been not the conquest of the Great Plains but the perfection of the Sabbath.

Some of the differences between the American and the Jewish historical experiences are general distinctions between secular and religious cultures. But if this is true the Jew living in America is all the better qualified to throw into sharp relief another striking feature of American life—its insistent secularity. Assuming, of course, that the existence and needs of the State of Israel do not give American Jewish life a secular character.

If Jews have lacked any clear distinction between

the secular and the religious realm (like that which
St. Augustine's *City of God* defined for the Christian tradition), this too fits them to hold up the
mirror to American civilization.

To overlook the distinctions in favor of the supposed similarities or identities of the Jewish and
the American historical experiences is to destroy
the peculiar qualifications of Jews as pupils, critics,
and mentors. This is, of course, not to say that
American Jews are any the less Americans because
they are Jews, but that if they would accept their
double inheritance they must also accept the
burden of an inner tension. In America of all places
they cannot refuse to be Double-men culturally.

"Our necessities," wrote Edgar Allen Poe of the
United States about a century ago, "have been
mistaken for our propensities. Having been forced
to make railroads, it has been deemed impossible
that we should make verse." Christianity (especially
Protestantism) in this country has proved comfortably responsive to these necessities; it has become permeated by the predominant character of
American culture to an extent which is not yet, and
may never be, true of Judaism. Christianity, simply
because it speaks for America, cannot so well speak
to America. May it not be that the American Jew—
stubbornly insoluble as he is—is providentially
fitted to distinguish the necessities from the possibilities of American culture?

ACKNOWLEDGMENTS

All except one of these essays were written during
the last six years. They are held together, if not by
a chain of argument, by a common quest for the
special character of American culture and American
history. "The Myth of an American Enlightenment" has not been published before. The others
appeared, in slightly different form, in the following publications. I wish to thank their editors and
publishers for permission to reprint.

The Foreword includes a revision of my talk on
receiving the Bancroft Prize of Columbia University on April 22, 1959, which appeared in *The
Columbia University Forum,* Fall 1959, Vol. 2, p.
49. "America and the Image of Europe," which
appeared in *Perspectives USA* No. 14, Winter 1956,
is reprinted by courtesy of Intercultural Publications, Inc. "The Place of Thought in American
Life" appeared in *The American Scholar,* Spring
1956, Vol. 25, pp. 137-50. "The Myth of an American Enlightenment" is a revision of an unpublished
paper entitled "History through Bifocal Glasses,"
given at a conference on the Present-Day Relevance

of Eighteenth-Century Thought held under the auspices of the American Council of Learned Societies at the Mayflower Hotel in Washington, D. C., on January 26, 1956. "An American Style in Historical Monuments" is a revision of "Past and Present in America: A Historian Visits Colonial Williamsburg," *Commentary*, January 1958, Vol. 25, pp. 1-7. "The Direct Democracy of Public Relations: Selling the President to the People" appeared as "Selling the President to the People: The Direct Democracy of Public Relations" in *Commentary*, November 1955, Vol. 20, pp. 421-7. "Some American Discontents" appeared as "Democracy and its Discontents" in *Encounter*, July 1954, Vol. 3, pp. 15-22. "Paths to National Self-Discovery: U.S.A. and Puerto Rico" appeared under the title "Self-Discovery in Puerto Rico" in *The Yale Review*, Winter 1956, Vol. 45, pp. 229-45, copyright Yale University Press. "A Dialogue of Two Histories: Jewish and American" appeared in *Commentary*, October 1949, Vol. 8, pp. 311-16.

In the collection and revision of these essays, I have had constant advice and editorial help from my wife, Ruth F. Boorstin, whose idea it was to produce such a volume as this, and who had already given immeasurable assistance in the writing of the articles when they first appeared. I also wish to thank Arthur A. Cohen and Aaron Asher of Meridian Books, Inc., for their acute editorial suggestions.

D. J. B.

October 1959